# SO
# CA

GW01464071

**By the staff of Editions Berlitz**

# How to use our guide

- All the practical information, hints and tips that you will need before and during the trip start on page 106, with a rundown of contents on page 109. Each island has its own Briefing Section at the end of each chapter, containing practical information specific to the island.

- For general background, see the sections The Islands and the People, p. 6, and A Brief History, p. 11.

- All the sights to see are listed between pages 16 and 81. Our own choice of sights most highly recommended is pinpointed by the Berlitz traveller symbol.

- Entertainment, nightlife and all other leisure activities are described between pages 82 and 98, while information on restaurants and cuisine is to be found on pages 98 to 105.

- Finally, there is an index at the back of the book, pp. 126–128.

---

*Although we make every effort to ensure the accuracy of all the information in this book, changes occur incessantly. We cannot therefore take responsibility for facts, prices, addresses and circumstances in general that are constantly subject to alteration. Our guides are updated on a regular basis as we reprint, and we are always grateful to readers who let us know of any errors, changes or serious omissions they come across.*

---

Text: Suzanne Patterson
Photography: Jürg Donatsch
We wish to thank the Eastern Caribbean Tourism Association, the Trinidad and Tobago Tourist Board, the Barbados Board of Tourism and the Grenada Tourist Board for their help in the preparation of this guide. We are also very grateful to BWIA, Mrs. Margo Bennett, Mr. Albert Haman and Mr. and Mrs. Norman Parkinson.

4  Cartography: Falk-Verlag, Hamburg.

# Contents

| | | |
|---|---|---|
| The Islands and the People | | 6 |
| A Brief History | | 11 |
| Where to Go | | 16 |
| | Barbados | 17 |
| | St. Lucia | 31 |
| | St. Vincent and the Grenadines | 41 |
| | Grenada | 52 |
| | Trinidad and Tobago | 61 |
| What to Do | | 82 |
| | Sports | 82 |
| | Shopping | 88 |
| | Entertainment | 92 |
| | Nightlife | 97 |
| Dining and Drinks | | 98 |
| How to Get There and When to Go | | 106 |
| Planning Your Budget | | 108 |
| **Blueprint for a Perfect Trip** (Practical Information) | | 109 |
| Index | | 126 |

**Maps**

| | | |
|---|---|---|
| | The Southern Caribbean | 9 |
| | Barbados | 19 |
| | St. Lucia | 33 |
| | St. Vincent and the Grenadines | 41 |
| | Grenada | 53 |
| | Trinidad | 63 |
| | Port-of-Spain | 66 |
| | Tobago | 74 |

# The Islands and the People

The Southern Caribbean islands are for escapists—who don't want to escape *too* far. They're not untouched Shangri-las waiting for a discoverer, but they have all the attributes. Lush tropical plants and flowers bloom year-round. Silvery, golden-white or volcanic black sand beaches fringe the turquoise Caribbean and indigo Atlantic. Wind-lashed and romantic, the Atlantic shores contrast with the gentle Caribbean.

Glorious sunshine and sunsets washed in every colour of a painter's palette add to the allure of the Southern Caribbean. The temperature seldom strays from the balmy range of 70° to 90° F. The rainy season officially extends from May to November, but showers rarely last very long. Hurricanes, fierce tropical storms that can sweep devastatingly through the Caribbean in late August and early September, pose the only real weather problem.

Getting away from it all is not difficult on these small islands*. They are strung out in an arc between the French West Indies and the Venezuelan coast—roughly 2,500 miles south of New York. Even the largest of them—Trinidad, with over 1,800 square miles —is a mite compared with Jamaica or Cuba to the north.

Trinidad bears a geological similarity to Venezuela, from which it broke away in the distant past. Tobago rose from the sea in volcanic eruptions, as did St. Lucia, St. Vincent and Grenada. Today, the volcanoes are mainly quiet tourist attractions, except for St. Vincent's which erupted dramatically in 1979. Barbados, the easternmost of the Southern Caribbean group, was

*Tropical rain forest meets the sea in an isolated palm-fringed cove.*

* Barbados, St. Lucia, St. Vincent, the Grenadines, Grenada, Tobago and Trinidad—referred to here for the sake of convenience as the Southern Caribbean islands. They share the same geographical situation within the West Indies, and none of them are more than 100 miles apart.

7

formed from deposits of coral and limestone, and this green and fertile isle always furnishes pure spring water.

Each island has its own distinctive history. Most of them were sighted by Christopher Columbus during his third voyage in 1498, but only Trinidad was claimed for Spain. It was the French and English who fought over and colonized the others, ousting the native Carib Indians in the process. This cannibal tribe waged a fierce battle for the area which now bears its name.

While pirates and buccaneers were creating havoc all over the Caribbean in the 18th

*Two young ladies of Trinidad beam a welcome to the visitor.*

century, sugar and slavery made rich planters of the adventurers who settled the islands. England gained the upper hand in the Southern Caribbean and eventually took all the islands for the Crown.

In the 19th century, slavery was abolished. Small landholdings were worked by former slaves, and the thirst for independence grew. The islands became British Associated States, but all of them have now chosen total independence and self-govern-

**8**

ment. Occasionally, there are political upheavals in these new nations, but events don't appear to disrupt local life.

About 90 per cent of the people who inhabit the Southern Caribbean islands are the black or mulatto descendants of African slaves. However, Trinidad's polyglot population includes East Indians and Chinese. St. Lucians converse in French patois, and the Barbadians have achieved a very high literacy rate.

Islanders express their creativity in music, Carnival costumes and an exuberant style of painting. Dancing is a way of life, and music can be heard everywhere, its sinuous rhythm inherited from Africa and influenced by Spain. Some islands boast excellent composers, songwriters, poets and playwrights. Trinidad-born V.S. Naipul, for one, has won international acclaim and many awards for his stories, essays and novels.

There are few high-rise developments in the Southern Caribbean, even on heavily populated Barbados. Wherever you look, you see brightly painted wooden houses with gingerbread ornament. Cars share road space with farm boys leading goats or carrying wicked-looking machetes for cutting sugar cane or chopping wood. Drivers take care to avoid swarms of little girls on their way home from school, adorable in cotton uniforms and neatly plaited hair.

An English-style school system is only one of the legacies left to the islands by Great Britain. Driving is on the left; everybody speaks English, and government and administration follow the British pattern. Cricket, tea and a general love of sport persist.

**THE SOUTHERN CARIBBEAN**

There are plenty of things to see and do in the islands. Visit the Great House of an old plantation or attend services in one of the islands' many churches Religious tolerance is taken for granted, especially on Trinidad, with its multiplicity of faiths. Botanic gardens are also a joy, with the right local guide.

Whether you holiday at one of the sophisticated resorts on Barbados, or claim a beach for your own on Tobago, you'll enjoy the pleasures of sun and sea. Cruise in your own tiny sailboat, climb to the peak of a volcanic mountain, or paddle the shallows in search of colourful fish.

Barbados boasts a vast new airport, and the island is fully geared to tourism. Others are moving at a somewhat slower pace. There are daily jet flights to a few islands and resort hotels on many of them, though the area is still relatively unspoiled. As for St. Lucia, St. Vincent and the Grenadines, you may have a beach to yourself, or nearly. So relax, and don't expect computer-rapid efficiency. Remember, you're in the tropics.

*St. Lucia's picturesque Castries market does a brisk daily business.*

# A Brief History

Long before Columbus set out on his voyages of discovery, groups of Amerindians made their way from South America to the Southern Caribbean area. By A.D. 300 tribes of Arawaks, peaceful farmers and fishermen, were in residence on many islands.

Then, a hundred years or so before the first Spanish adventurers arrived, a warlike tribe swept up from South America, killing off the Arawaks and probably eating their flesh for ritualistic purposes, if not for food.

They called themselves *caribes* (rendered in Spanish as *canibales*—"cannibals"), but the savage name later came to be given to the gentlest of turquoise seas and lushest of islands. The Caribs founded settlements on most of the Southern Caribbean islands, and it was they who invented the hammock—a device adopted by the Spanish and many a weary jet-age traveller.

**Exploration and Colonization**
Columbus sighted most of the Southern Caribbean islands on his third voyage in 1498, remarking on their beauty and then sailing on. Soon other

Spaniards were in hot pursuit of treasure, real and imagined. They concentrated on Cuba, Mexico and the South American mainland, using the Southern Caribbean islands principally as bases from which to search for the gold of El Dorado.

Only Trinidad was colonized by Spain, and the exploitation of the smaller islands was left to the British and French. By the early 16th century, the French, English and Dutch had staked claims in the Southern Caribbean, bringing Spanish dominance of the area to an end. In the 1510s sugar cane was introduced into most of the islands, as well as a small trade in slaves, which was soon cornered by the Portuguese.

Not content with the establishment of embryonic colonies, the French and British also indulged in smuggling and privateering—the appropriation of goods from ships of rival countries with the blessings of the home government. Throughout the 16th and 17th centuries, buccaneers from France and Great Britain plundered the region.

*A dignified Columbus presides over Port-of-Spain, Trinidad.*

CRISTOFORO COLONBO

In 1562, an English privateer called John Hawkins broke the Portuguese monopoly on slave-trading by bringing slaves from the West African coast and selling them in the Caribbean. Shortly after that, in 1586, Sir Francis Drake (who was knighted as much for buccaneering as other naval exploits) sacked the town of Cartagena in Colombia in the name of the English Crown. Two years later, he and John Hawkins led forces to defeat the Spanish Armada, an event that marked Spain's gradual decline as a strong influence in the New World.

On the islands, the 17th century saw a boom in the production of sugar cane, which was cultivated intensively from about 1650 onwards, and the manufacture of rum. As refining mills were built, more and more slaves were imported from Africa—as many as 75,000 a year by the end of the 17th century. During the heyday of the sugar plantations, when the Great Houses, with their refinements and fine furniture, flourished, the slaves were secretly mutinous, expressing discontent in their music and dance, a portent of rebellion to come. Their black descendants would later rule most of the Caribbean.

## Britain vs. France

Except for Barbados, which never strayed from the British fold, the Southern Caribbean islands changed hands many times as the British and French struggled for dominance. The Seven Years' War waged by the two powers for supremacy in North America ended in 1763 with the loss to France of Canada and several Caribbean islands—all ceded to Great Britain by the Treaty of Paris. Not long afterwards, the French reclaimed some islands, most of them only temporarily. The strife grew more intense during the American Revolution, when France sided with American rebels against Great Britain.

In 1782 the British under Admiral George Rodney defeated the French in the Battle of the Saints. The next year, by terms of the Treaty of Versailles, St. Vincent and Grenada were returned to Great Britain. This time Britannia ruled for nearly two centuries. St. Lucia, however, went to the French, Rodney's protests notwithstanding.

Due to the 1789 revolution and its aftermath, the French were losing their grip on the Caribbean. By the Treaty of Amiens (1802), Trinidad (captured by the British in 1797) **13** was formally ceded to Great Britain. St. Lucia was transferred to the English in 1814 at the end of the Napoleonic Wars.

## Towards Independence

Enlightened thought in France and England condemned slavery and encouraged revolutions like the one on Hispaniola in 1791. Toussaint L'Ouverture, a former slave, eventually turned part of that island into the world's first black democracy—a country called Haiti. England outlawed slave-trading in 1807, followed by the French in 1818. Slavery itself was abolished in all British colonies in 1833, taking effect the next year. The French followed suit in 1848.

But there was no one to plough the fields. New labour was needed, especially on Trinidad, and tens of thousands of workers were brought to the island from India, creating a population of differing colours and religions. The cultural impact was considerable.

Although the early 20th century was an era of self-expression and nationalism elsewhere in the Caribbean, the southern islands stayed under the aegis of Great Britain until the 1960s, and most of them did not gain complete independence until the late seventies. The expansion of American influence during and after World War II affected only Trinidad, an oil-refining country of strategic importance, where U.S. bases were constructed.

Attempts have been made at unified Caribbean government and administration. But no matter how small, the island nations rarely agree, and the most they have achieved is a vague cooperative economic community, CARICOM.

While the former British islands are firmly self-governing today, the atmosphere remains British, with parliamentary governments and administrations firmly based on British models. But each island has its individuality, qualities and problems. Throughout the Southern Caribbean governments have discovered that—with agriculture and small industries—they have a huge economic resource in tourism, which continues to grow by leaps and bounds.

Some islands are more far-sighted than others, building

*On Trinidad tradition and technology converge, as oxen and cranes team up for the sugar cane harvest.*

efficient airports with the help of outside capital and aiding the tourist with a minimum of bureaucracy. On these islands you'll find plenty of new shops and luxury resort hotels. Others remain relatively untouched by the tourist explosion, offering visitors unspoiled landscapes and bountiful hospitality. Both more than make up for the material inconveniences.

Those who love the small Southern Caribbean islands fervently hope that future development will not detract from their outstanding natural beauty, nor from the dignity of their people.

# Where to Go

All of the islands in the Southern Caribbean lie roughly within 30 minutes to one hour of one another by air. Barbados boasts a huge modern airport and serves as the main port of entry to the area. In addition, the tourist industry is highly developed, and there's plenty to see and do.

Frequent flights link Barbados to St. Lucia, 100 miles to the north-west, and there are also some direct international air connections. Relaxation and friendship with a French flavour highlight a visit to St. Lucia.

St. Vincent, 21 miles south of St. Lucia, can be reached by air or boat. The island, a pleasant holiday destination in itself, also makes a logical starting point for downwind yacht tours of the Grenadines. You can also travel by scheduled service between St. Vincent, the idyllic Grenadines, and Grenada—a strikingly beautiful island with exceptional beaches.

Oil-rich Trinidad has beautiful island scenery, though industrial development has taken its toll of the landscape. It is generally easier to travel to Trinidad by jet or small plane, rather than by scheduled boat service. The Carnival season is undoubtedly the most exciting time to visit.

It's usually more satisfactory to fly to the easy-going resort island of Tobago, as the boat journey from Trinidad can be uncomfortable. Good bathing, tranquillity and scenic beauty bring tourists back to the island year after year.

We cover the islands in counter-clockwise order, starting with Barbados.

**16**

# Barbados

Barbados lies outside the main island chain, about 100 miles to the east of St. Vincent in the path of the cooling trade winds. This small, pear-shaped island teems with 260,000 inhabitants—though you're rarely aware of crowds, except on a shopping day in Bridgetown, the capital. Barbados is highly civilized and as British as tea-time; not that there isn't plenty of tropical beauty. Pristine Caribbean beaches are edged with palms and the windswept Atlantic coast with its high cliffs has a rugged appeal.

Unlike the volcanic islands.

*Barbadians and tourists alike take to the waters of the soothing Caribbean or the bracing Atlantic—wild, windswept and rugged.*

Barbados is capped by limestone and coral, which means that when rain falls (more than you'd think), it's trapped underground to be drawn in a pure state from wells.

Barbados extends a welcome as warm as the climate, and you'll find the people friendly and genuinely helpful. Accommodation ranges from simple beach huts to luxury resorts that rival the world's best. Everything is geared to help the tourist relax, and you won't find a more comprehensive array of sports facilities anywhere in the Caribbean. Modern music and lively entertainment keep night-owls amused till dawn, and many people from other islands come over to join in the fun.

Roads are acceptable, and you can easily drive yourself around the island. However, it's a good idea to take a semi-private tour or hire a taxi to guide you around at first. Guides and drivers will tell you that Barbados is divided into 11 parishes—St. James's, Christ Church, St. Michael's, etc. It's confusing at first, but after a few days you'll know that Bridgetown is in St. Michael's, resort development centres around Christ Church and the Platinum Coast beaches are in St. James's.

## Historical Highlights

Barbados maintains closer ties to England than any other Southern Caribbean island. Nearly 350 years of British rule produced no hard feelings on either side, and many Barbadians are ardent Anglophiles. British visitors will detect in their charming hybrid accent something of the Midlands—and a hint of a soft Scottish brogue.

Barbados was sighted by a Portuguese explorer, Pedro a Campos, in 1536. He called the island *los Barbudos* ("the bearded ones") after the hoary-looking banyan trees whose hanging roots resembled beards. But Pedro made no claims on Barbados. A century later, in 1625, an English ship touched land at Jamestown, later named Holetown. Once the island had been claimed for Britain, there were no invasions by rival powers, a record for this part of the world.

Soon Barbados boasted tobacco, cotton and sugar cane plantations, with stills for the manufacture of rum. Slaves were introduced to work the cane fields, and by 1666 the black population numbered 50,000, compared to 8,000 English slave owners. On Barbados slaves were treated relatively well, and there were no bloody uprisings to compare with other islands to the north, such as Haiti.

Today's white population shares a complex ancestry of former masters and indentured servants, political prisoners and free-thinkers from Ireland and Scotland—jailbirds who dared to try a bit of crime or even a new religion.

Although politically peaceful through the centuries, plague, yellow fever and hurri-

canes sporadically ravaged the island. Nevertheless, Barbados flourished, especially as an attractive holiday destination. One early tourist, George Washington, paid a visit in 1751 with his half-brother, Lawrence, ill with consumption.

In the 17th and 18th centuries, planters built elegant Great Houses with breezy verandahs overlooking immaculately trimmed gardens.

After the abolition of slavery in 1833, Barbados gradual-

**BARBADOS**

North Point
Animal Flower Cave
Crab Hill
Great Head
ST. LUCY
Nicholas Abbey
Cherry Tree Hill
850ft.
Morgan Lewis
Farley
Windmill
Six Men's Bay
Hill
Speightstown
ST. PETER
ST. ANDREW
Scotland
Chalky
District
Mount
ST JAMES
Bathsheba
Andromeda
Gardens
ST. JOSEPH
St. John's
Welchman
Church
Conset Bay
Holetown
Hall Gully
Harrison's
Codrington College
Sandy Lane Bay
Cave
ST. JOHN
Payne's Bay
ST. THOMAS
Ashford
Villa
Ragged
Bird Park
Nova
Point
ST. MICHAEL
ST. GEORGE
ST. PHILIP
Paradise
Beach
Bulkeley
Sam Lord's Castle
Deep Water Harbour
Crane Beach
**Bridgetown**
Barbados
Museum
CHRIST CHURCH
Garrison
Hastings
Mystery Vault
Savannah
St.Lawrence
Oistin
Maxwell
Oistins
Long Bay
Bay

ATLANTIC OCEAN

N

0   2   4   6 km
0       2       4 miles

ly moved towards independence. Its parliament, founded in 1639, is the third oldest in the British Commonwealth. The island achieved full independence within the Commonwealth in 1966, as well as becoming a member of the United Nations. Barbados is considered one of the most stable island-nations in the Caribbean, perhaps due in part to an exceptionally high literacy rate of 98 per cent.

## Bridgetown

Today's bustling centre of commerce and seagoing activity was officially founded by the Earl of Carlisle in 1628. The capital probably takes its name from an old Indian bridge that is said to have spanned the River Constitution. Bear in mind that Bridgetown streets can be very hot and crowded about noon; try to visit the town early in the day.

Start your tour in **Trafalgar Square,** a bustling plaza at the centre of city activity. Taxis and buses usually stop nearby in Broad Street, a colourful thoroughfare with old colonial buildings, including shops packed with duty-free bargains. In the square you'll see a dignified bronze monument to Lord Nelson, erected in honour of the admiral in 1813. Although London's famous memorial may be bigger, Bridgetown's was the first by many years. Here, too, stands "The Fountain", erected in the 1860s to commemorate the introduction of a piped water system.

Just north of the square, you'll notice the quaint neo-Gothic **Public Buildings,** constructed to house the Barbados legislature after a fire in 1860 destroyed most of the neighbourhood. Little streets leading from the Public Buildings to Swan Street contain old and new examples of Barbados architecture.

Across Chamberlain Bridge, you'll see the **Careenage**—a shallow inlet where boats are careened (from a French expression for "to turn over") for repair, caulking and painting. Banana boats and fishing dinghies fill the harbour, along with replicas of the proud galleons that roamed the Caribbean two centuries ago; they sail again, pressed into service on sightseeing cruises. In the area you may see harbour policemen dressed in tradi-

*The bold paintwork of Bridgetown shines bright in the tropical sun.*

ANGEL HEART

tional uniforms of midshipman's blouse and bell-bottomed trousers unchanged since Nelson's day.

Walk in a north-easterly direction past the bus terminus to **Fairchild Market,** where sellers tempt passers-by with the luscious tropical produce of Barbados and neighbouring islands. The market is at its liveliest early in the morning when fruit and vegetables are at their freshest.

From here take O'Neal Bridge to Trafalgar Street and St. Michael's Row, the site of **St. Michael's Cathedral.** This typical Caribbean-style Anglican edifice dates from 1831. The self-appointed guides will tell you more than you want to know about the coral-rock structure with wooden choir stalls and galleries. While Barbados has churches of many denominations, Anglican still predominates.

Up the road from St. Michael's you come to **Queen's**

**Park,** an elegant pink-and-white residence that housed the British Commanding General until the beginning of this century. Now art exhibitions are held here; the adjacent park boasts an enormous baobab tree that measures over 60 feet in circumference.

To the east lies the **Belleville** district, a residential area full of pretty Victorian houses, and **Government House,** the residence of the Governor General, the representative of the English Crown. The venerable mansion dates from the early 18th century, making it one of the oldest buildings on the island.

Big cruise ships put in at the Deep Water Harbour, situated about a mile from the centre of Bridgetown. A tourist office has been established nearby for the convenience of cruise passengers. Also in the vicinity is the Pelican Crafts Village, established in 1958 to promote local handiwork and worth a short visit.

The **Garrison Savannah,** former British military headquarters, lies on the southern outskirts of town. A race track and playing fields are situated on the old parade grounds, and the military prison now houses the **Barbados Museum.** Don't fail to see this gem of the Caribbean. Scattered about the grassy courtyard are sugar moulds, penny-farthing bicycles and ships' anchors. Gallery exhibits highlight local lore, seashells, fish and Arawak culture. There is a special display of prints relating to the islands, as well as fine English furniture. The museum build-

*Escape on a "buccaneer" boat: a relaxed way to see Barbados' coast.* **23**

ings even preserve a neat but dreary prison cell.

**St. Ann's Fort** close by dates from the early years of the 18th century. The fortification, with its conspicuous clock tower, has become a local landmark.

## Atlantic Sights

The rugged Atlantic coast merits at least a short visit. Take the coast road from Bridgetown to the pleasant resorts of HASTINGS, ST. LAWRENCE, MAXWELL and OISTINS BAY; or travel inland through green sugar cane country, past little churches and tiny towns with gingerbread houses. You may want to visit the Christ Church parish church above Oistins, with its puzzling **"Mystery Vault"**. During the last century, the coffins contained here were said to have changed position, and to this day the mystery has never been solved.

As you approach the southeast, the sea grows more agitated and steep white headlands plunge down to the shore. Admire the windswept and dramatic view from **Crane Beach,** where good surfing awaits the brave.

Somewhat farther to the north-east is **Sam Lord's Castle,** a hotel that happens to be a prime tourist attraction. For a small admission fee you can visit the old plantation house, beautifully decorated with furniture of Barbados mahogany made locally in the Regency style. Much of the china and many of the portraits on display were spoils taken from ships wrecked on the rocks offshore by the legendary Sam Lord, who is said to have hung lanterns from the cliffs to lure the ships onto the shallow reef. The house itself looks like a

*Tourists trace the footsteps of the notorious Sam Lord, wrecker of the Barbados coast. His "castle", a monumental Great House, is now a hotel.*

Georgian architectural hybrid, but the rooms are nicely proportioned and the site is incomparable.

Continue north along the east coast to CONSET BAY, then head inland past Codrington College, one of the oldest schools in the Western hemisphere (1745). There are several points of interest in the St. John's area. **Villa Nova,** a dignified old plantation Great House, is still privately owned and can only be seen from the verandah. Beautiful furnishings enhance the light and airy house, while gardens and grounds are kept up to tropical par.

Close by at **Ashford Bird Park,** another plantation Great **25**

House set in a large park, you're guided around by members of the owner's family. The main attraction is the excellent collection of exotic birds and animals which includes the flamboyantly coloured lory and Barbados monkeys from the surrounding hills.

**St. John's Church,** perched 825 feet above sea level, offers lovely views of the St. John's area. The present structure dates back to 1836, and the cemetery, older still, contains the mossy grave of Ferdinando Paleologus, a possible descendant of the Byzantine emperors.

Now follow the coast road north to picturesque **Bathsheba** (with the accent on the first syllable), where small pastel houses cling gallantly to chalky cliffs that rise high above the

*Orchids grow like wild flowers in Andromeda Gardens, on Barbados.*

raging Atlantic. Holidaying Barbadians flock to the wild and windy Bathsheba region because it is less expensive, less frequented and cooler than the other shores in summer.

Be sure to visit **Andromeda Gardens,** a must on any east coast tour. This privately owned botanical garden contains dozens of varieties of flowers, plants and trees. Among them is the shaggy bearded banyan tree that inspired the name "Barbados".

From Bathsheba the coast road becomes narrow and dangerous in places, but you'll enjoy the view, especially from **The Potteries** a village of ceramic craftsmen situated on the summit of CHALKY MOUNT at the healthy altitude of 571 feet. Look for a nearby land formation called "Napoleon", which resembles a man lying on his back with his hands across his stomach. You can also see the green and rugged hills of the SCOTLAND district, named for its resemblance to the European country and still populated by a few "Redlegs", as the original inhabitants were known.

Return to Bridgetown via GUN HILL in St. George's parish, the site of a former signal station that communicated messages to St. Ann's Fort.

The lion carved out of a rock jutting from the hillside was the work of a British soldier. Nearby, St. George's Church, an 18th-century edifice, preserves an **altarpiece** of the Resurrection from the same century by the American, Benjamin West.

## The Platinum Coast

The west coast takes its name from the brilliant white of its sandy beaches. Many luxury hotels and big private mansions are situated along this "Millionaire's Row". Nevertheless, between the resort developments and imposing estates, you can still see wooden Barbadian houses with their gingerbread decoration.

Heading west from Bridgetown, you pass scenic PARADISE BEACH in St. James's parish. The turquoise water grows clearer and the beaches whiter as you progress towards PAYNE'S BAY and SANDY LANE BAY, a favourite haunt of film stars and the English Royal Family. In HOLETOWN, a monument commemorates the founding of Barbados' first settlement by Englishmen from the ship *Olive Branch.* However, the date inscribed here, 1605, predates the actual landing by some 20 years. The Anglican **St. James's Church.** 27

founded in 1660 and rebuilt in 1874, preserves a 17th-century font and a large bell inscribed "God Bless King William, 1696".

Drive inland a short distance from Holetown to **Welchman Hall Gully.** This vast tropical forest, now running wild, was originally a spice plantation. You can still see nutmeg, cinnamon and fruit trees among the lush lianas and parasite vines. The walk through the grounds can take a good half-hour or so, even at a brisk clip.

Nearby is **Harrison's Cave** where a special tram will take you down through an exciting cavern of stalagmites and stalactites.

Return to the coast and travel north again to **Speights-town** (pronounced "spite"), once the sugar capital of the north-west area. The town was known as "Little Bristol", since the Speight family did most of their trade with the English port. Speightstown has remained typically West Indian, with small, pastel wooden houses and shops, old churches and an easygoing populace greeting one another in the streets. Just north at SIX MEN'S BAY, old cannon are ranged about the silvery shore, another picturesque reminder of the past.

Continue north through flat sugar-cane country to NORTH POINT and **Animal Flower Cave,** where a willing guide will lead you down steep steps to a cavern carved out by the sea. You'll see coral rock tinted every colour of the rainbow and the animal flower itself—an exquisite, tentacled sea anemone that recoils when you touch it. Don't forget to bring rubber-soled shoes. Phone the Tourism Board to check that high waves have not temporarily closed the cave.

On the return journey, take the road that winds through St. Lucy's parish to CHERRY TREE HILL (850 feet). There are no cherry trees in sight, only mahogany, the robust tree that was first planted on the island in 1763.

**Farley Hill,** once a venerable plantation house, lies a short distance away over a road with many turns. Many royal visitors were entertained here, including King George V, and the house was the setting for the film *Island in the Sun.* Today Farley Hill is little more than a ruin, though the bright hibiscus and poinsettia that grow all around the crumbling walls add a touch of cheer. Take a walk over the green lawns and admire a fine view of the Scotland district.

*Oblique view of a venerable relic: old windmill recalls days when sugar was king of the islands.*

**Nicholas Abbey,** another plantation house in the area, delights visitors with its Persian arches and well-kept gardens. A short distance east stands the **Morgan Lewis Windmill,** a rather forlorn reminder of the days when sugar-making was introduced by Dutch settlers from Brazil. They soon left sugar cultivation to the British, however. To return to Bridgetown, take Highway 2, an inland route that is also the most direct. **29**

# Barbados Briefing

**Airport.** Grantley Adams International Airport is the most modern and efficient airport in the Southern Caribbean area with bank, restaurant, bar, tourist information service, car-hire agencies, public telephones, several duty-free shops and postal facilities. It is completely air-conditioned. The airport is about 11 miles from the capital. Bus service is inexpensive, and some hotels fetch guests in mini-buses. On leaving Barbados, visitors must pay a departure tax.

**Currency.** Barbados dollar (BD$), 100 cents = BD$1. Issued in 1, 5, 10, 20 and 100-dollar notes, and coins of 1, 5, 10 and 25 cents and 1 dollar.

**Electric current.** 110 volts, 50 cycle AC. Various plug systems are in use, from American to British, though the British 3-prong system is coming into favour.

**Emergencies.** Dial 112 for police, 113 for fire, 426-1113 for ambulance.

**Hospitals.** Queen Elizabeth General Hospital, Bridgetown, tel. 426-0930, and St. Joseph Hospital, St. Peter, tel. 422-2232.

**Hours.** *Business and shopping hours* are generally 8 a.m. to 4 or 5 p.m. weekdays. On Saturday shops open from 8 a.m. to noon. *Banks:* Monday to Thursday 8 a.m. 1 or 3 p.m., Friday 8 a.m. to 1 p.m. and 3 to 5 or 5.30 p.m.

**Newspapers.** The *Barbados Advocate* and the *Nation* are published daily; magazines for tourists include the *Bajan* and the *Visitor*.

**Public Holidays.** New Year's Day (January 1), Good Friday and Easter Monday (movable), Labour Day (May 1), Whit Monday (movable), Kadooment Day (first Monday in July), Caribbean Community Day (first Monday in August), United Nations Day (first Monday in October), Independence Day (November 30), Christmas Day and Boxing Day (December 25 and 26).

## Tourist Information Offices

*Barbados:* Barbados Board of Tourism, Prescod Boulevard & Harbour Road, P.O. Box 242, Bridgetown, tel. 427-2623, and at the airport

*Canada:* Barbados Board of Tourism, Suite 1508, Box 11, 20 Queen Street West, Toronto, Ont. M5H 3R3, tel. (416) 979-2137/38

*U.K.:* Barbados Board of Tourism, 6, Upper Belgrave Street, London SW1, tel. (01) 235-4607

*U.S.A.:* Barbados Board of Tourism, 800 Second Avenue, New York, NY 10017, tel. (212) 986-6516

# St. Lucia

This beautiful volcanic island midway between Martinique and St. Vincent boasts some of the best scenery in the Caribbean—rugged green jungles, undulating agricultural land, dazzling beaches and the volcanic, cone-shaped Pitons. There's even a dormant but still bubbling volcano called Soufrière that can be viewed from inside without danger.

Francophiles love St. Lucia for its French atmosphere. Many place-names are French —from the capital, Castries, to Vieux Fort on the southern tip of the island. Most of the 124,000 inhabitants converse in French patois and can understand, if not speak, some basic French.

*Idyllic days on St. Lucia: tranquil waters of Marigot Bay, ideal for mooring, perfect for a swim.*

## Native Patois

On St. Lucia everybody speaks English and most people understand French. But among themselves, islanders converse in patois, a dialect based on French. However, the syntax differs from French, genders are often dropped and the letter "r" sounds more like "w". Negatives are made by putting "pa" (like the French *pas*) before a verb. Needless to say, only a practised ear can understand it.

| It is not mine. | Sé pa sa-mwē. | *Say pa sam-wehng* |
| How much is it? | Kōmē i kuté? | *Kong mehng ee koo-tay* |
| What a pretty place. | Mi yō bèl coté. | *Mee yong behl ko-tay* |

While St. Lucia (pronounced LOO-sha) remains agricultural, with bananas the most important crop, islanders keep an attentive eye on tourism. You can be very comfortable here, and there are provisions for all sorts of summer sports. Enjoy good music every night and indulge in the excellent native cuisine, with its coconuts, bananas and tropical spices.

## Historical Highlights

Carib Indians had St. Lucia more or less to themselves until the early 17th century, when a group of Englishmen from a ship called the *Olive Blossom* landed and tried to set up a colony. Within a span of weeks, however, the Caribs had killed most of them. Again, in 1639, there was an abortive 18-month attempt by some Englishmen to colonize the island, but they, too, were driven off by the Caribs.

The French were eyeing beautiful and strategically placed St. Lucia as well; so began a tug-of-war history in which St. Lucia was constantly changing hands between French and English. In 1765, during one brief French reign, the first sugar plantation was started and small towns were built up; but trouble began as the American and French Revolutions spread to the West Indies. The Treaty of Amiens returned St. Lucia to France in 1802, but the British reclaimed it.

The British finally prevailed and the 19th century—an era of coconut, sugar cane, coffee and cotton plantations—was largely a peaceful time. Emancipation was met with ecstasy by former slaves, creating a few administrative problems.

St. Lucia went forward gradually towards self-government, which was granted with the West Indies Act in 1967. After a period of quibbles, upsets and mild instability caused by a tug-of-war between the leading political parties, the island has returned to its usual state of calm.

## Castries

The capital was named in 1785 after the Maréchal de Castries, then Minister of Marine responsible for the French colonies. However, few buildings remain from the 18th century, mainly due to two devastating fires which swept the town in 1948 and 1951. Today's city of about 45,000 inhabitants looks frankly jerry-built, though some quarters have a certain charm.

Take a look at the scenic **yacht basin** (in a defunct volcano crater) and the lively **harbour,** site of a fish market late in the afternoon. Just across the way, the **market** for food and charcoal, which is used for cooking fuel, hums with activity in the morning. You'll see plenty of island produce for sale, the array varying with the season.

**ST. LUCIA**

Along Bridge Street, you'll find the central post office and the largest shops. Spacious **Columbus Square,** one of the capital's few picturesque corners, boasts tropical greenery, and a samman tree and a huge mahogany cast their shade. The 19th-century Catholic **cathedral** has interesting wooden columns, iron vaulting and frescoes painted by a pupil of the French artist Puvis de Chavannes. Opposite the cathedral stands the most

*The faithful of Castries pray at the altar of their ornate cathedral.*

handsome building in town, the **Central Library.** This red-and-white structure of stucco and stone, named officially after its benefactors, the Carnegies of America, looks older than it is (19th century).

Castries may lack charm, but the capital is backed up by its own mountain, Morne For-

tuné, and what could be more romantic than a name that means "Sad Mountain With Luck"? A drive to the top up precipitous roads leads to 18th-century **Fort Charlotte,** an unremarkable military installation with good views. Both French and British conducted their squabbles from the ramparts.

In the middle of the 19th century, three military buildings were erected on Morne Fortuné. The buildings have been restored and now form part of the island's principal educational complex. But you can still see many reminders of the British and French forces who fought each other for St. Lucia. From this hill you also have a sweeping view of Castries harbour, Vigie peninsula, Pigeon Island and the Pitons.

## Towards the North

Many of the island's luxury hotels are situated to the north of Castries along a road as good as it is scenic. The hotels are friendly places and they admit non-residents for drinks, meals or a swim. In the area are sparkling crescent-shaped beaches, as VIGIE BEACH, CHOC BEACH and GROS ISLET.

A causeway links **Pigeon Island** to the mainland. The islet, remarkable for its high, green hill, finds favour with energetic climbers. Bring a picnic lunch and settle down for awhile to enjoy the beautiful views of Martinique to the north. The island was the main base of Admiral Rodney in the 18th century, and the name "pigeon" probably comes from Rodney's hobby of breeding the birds. Today the abandoned grey stone barracks once used by the British garrison looks like a haunted villa. The barracks, together with a museum, is situated within the national park that has been developed on Pigeon Point.

North of Pigeon Island, scenery turns rocky and weather breezy, but the cool, green hill region has attracted entrepreneurs. Land in CAP ESTATE is being snapped up by foreigners, and the northern area has been developed with yacht basins, some shops, a hotel and a golf course.

## Exploring the South

Soufrière volcano and the Pitons are not to be missed on any visit to St. Lucia. You can reach these spectacular sights either by boat on a pleasant day's cruise, by organized tour or car. It's wise to hire a driver familiar with all the hair-raising bends. The circular coastal road that travels around the southern two-thirds of the island was established in the 18th century by the Maréchal de Laborie.

Just south of Castries, you

pass CUL DE SAC, an aptly named sheltered harbour lined with banana plants—St. Lucia's biggest agricultural product. Next comes MARIGOT BAY, a secluded and still idyllic palm-fringed spot with several hotels and restaurants. Farther along are more attractive and isolated bays and beaches: ANSE LA RAYE, where local people make boats from gum trees and sails from flour bags; ANSE COCHON (French for pig) and the little fishing village of CANARIES.

By land or by sea, the sight of the cone-shaped **Pitons** will take your breath away. Postcards give no more than an idea of the majestic beauty of these volcanic mountains—the Gros Piton (2,619 ft.) and the Petit Piton (2,460 ft.).

**Soufrière town,** typically West Indian with brightly painted arcaded buildings, nestles just under the twin mountains. Unspoiled as it looks, the locals have seen all too many tour groups. Although official guides and the police formally discourage begging, you may be assailed by self-styled guides, palms extended for money, or little boys who forget school to dive naked for coins.

Follow the road leading to

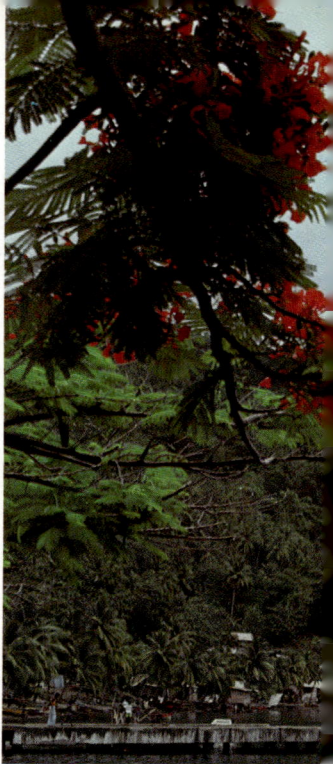

**36** the renovated **sulphur baths,** situated just outside town. The baths were discovered by the French, and in 1784, Maréchal de Laborie, then in command of the island, sent samples of the water to Paris. They were analyzed by Louis XVI's doctors, who pronounced the source to be beneficial. The water gurgles and steams in a jungle setting of dense vegetation. You're welcome to take a dip, perhaps in the company of a group of shy schoolgirls.

A path leads through the tropical forest to the source. Don't plunge your hand into the water; it is boiling hot and can burn. If you walk farther along the path, beyond the

*The spectacular twin cones of the Pitons loom over little Soufrière.*

hottest part of the source, you come to a lovely waterfall and pond. Do *not* wade or bathe here. This is a known breeding ground for the highly dangerous bilharzia parasite.

**37**

From the baths take the twisting road to **Soufrière,** advertised as the world's only drive-in volcano. And so it is. The road goes right up to the crater, steaming away like an inferno. Competent guides lead you quickly over the hot stones and through the noxious sulphur gases to an untouchable black pit where the steaming water reaches 212 °F. Efforts are being made to harness the steam energy—360 pounds per square inch—for island use. Note that some rocks are coloured green by copper deposits, white by lime and chalk and yellow by sulphur.

In case you're apprehensive, remember that nobody worries about this dormant volcano erupting violently, since anything that lets off steam to such an extent probably won't blow up for a while. This line of reasoning may not be scientific, but it sounds convincing to anybody who has done some cooking.

Again take the road south and make for CHOISEUL and LABORIE, two ramshackle but picturesque little villages surrounded by splendid vegeta-

*Bubble, bubble, but no toil or trouble to see the drive-in volcano.*

tion. You'll see men with machetes harvesting crops of bananas, cocoa, citrus fruit, coconuts, peanuts, sweet potatoes or cabbage, depending on the season.

The road levels out as it reaches VIEUX FORT and Hewanorra Airport, the island's largest. The airport's name has its origin in a Carib word meaning "Land of the Iguana". Iguanas, large lizards that are harmless unless attacked, have dwindled in number on the island. You're unlikely to see one, unless you climb a mountain or stay at one of the hotels that keep a pet iguana in a cage.

A picturesque lighthouse stands on MOULE À CHIQUE cape. On a clear day the view from the cape is spectacular. If you look out to sea, you'll glimpse the island of St. Vincent. Look inland, across St. Lucia, and you'll see the Pitons. The seemingly endless Atlantic. beach that stretches north of the cape is well whipped by winds and decorated with a glossy commercial hotel.

As you travel up the east coast, you'll find the circular road somewhat easier going, not that there isn't plenty to keep a driver alert—whether children on their way home from school or cows, donkeys and sheep wandering on the road. Headlands project into the ocean, and there are two little towns to explore, MICOUD and Dennery. Inland, midway between them, rises Mt. Gimie, the highest point on the island at 3,117 feet.

Dennery earned renown as a den of iniquity, and until the 1950s a part of town called Oléon (or Aux Lyons) was closed to outsiders. Townspeople made a strong (and illegal) local brew known as *mal cochon*, and they were so belligerent in the defense of their privacy that even the police were reluctant to interfere.

Roads don't travel inland on St. Lucia, but guides can lead you over the hills and through the jungle if you're willing to hike. Although a few deadly *fer-de-lance* snakes inhabit the tropical forest, you're unlikely to see one; and the trip is worthwhile for the animal and bird life you encounter, including the colourful, blue-headed St. Lucia parrot.

From Dennery the circular road winds gradually back across the island in the direction of LA TOC and Castries. To reach the capital, you cross through the flat Cul de Sac plantation and up a mountain road with good sea views.

## St. Lucia Briefing

**Airports.** St. Lucia has two airports. Hewanorra Airport, the larger of the two, is at the southern end of the island (about 38 miles from the capital and most hotels). The airport has small duty-free shops, car-hire agencies, a postbox and a tourist information office, but is not air-conditioned. There is an air link to the other airport, Vigie, conveniently situated near most of the better hotels. Customs is informal, and there is usually someone from the tourist office on hand, as well as a car-hire agency representative. Small planes from Hewanorra and the other islands land here. Both airports levy a departure tax.

**Currency.** Eastern Caribbean dollar (EC$), 100 cents = EC$1. Notes: EC$ 1, 5, 20 and 100. Coins: 1, 2, 5, 10, 25, 50 cents and EC$1.

**Electric current.** 220/230 volts, 50 cycle AC. Some hotels have 110-volt outlets in rooms. The British 3-prong plug system is in use.

**Emergencies.** Dial 999 for police, ambulance or fire.

**Hospitals:** Victoria Hospital, Castries, tel. 22421. St. Jude's Hospital, Vieux Fort, tel. 46041.

**Hours.** *Business and shopping:* 8 a.m. to 12.30 p.m. and 1.30 to 4 p.m. Monday to Friday, Saturday 8 a.m. to noon. *Banking hours:* 8 a.m. to noon or 1 p.m. Monday to Thursday, Friday 8 a.m. to noon and 3 to 5 p.m.

**Newspapers.** The *Voice* is published twice a week, the *Crusader* on Saturdays.

**Public Holidays.** New Year's Days (January 1 and 2), Good Friday and Easter Monday (March/April), Whit Monday (May/June), Corpus Christi (June), Queen's Birthday (June), Bank Holiday (August), Thanksgiving Day (October), National Day (December 13th), Christmas Day and Boxing Day (December 25 and 26).

### Tourist Information Offices

*St. Lucia:* St. Lucia Tourist Board, Northern Wharf, P.O. Box 221, Castries, tel. 45-25968.

*Canada:* St. Lucia Tourist Board, 151 Bloor Street West, Suite 425, Toronto, Ont. M5S 1S4, tel. (416) 961-5606.

*U.K.:* See Eastern Caribbean Tourist Association, page 51.

*U.S.A.:* St. Lucia Tourist Board, 41 East 42nd Street, Suite 315, New York, NY 10017, tel. (212) 867-2950.

# St. Vincent and the Grenadines

Constant and intense volcanic activity through the ages has endowed St. Vincent with a fringe of shiny black-sand beaches, notably on the Atlantic side. Bleakly spectacular, they contrast with the lush terraced hills inland. The island's 133 square miles form a rough ellipse with a bump on the western side. Soufrière volcano bubbles out of the narrower northern end, and unlike St. Lucia's, this one still erupts. During periods of volcanic activity, ash has been spewed as far as Barbados, 100 miles to the east.

Aside from problems caused by volcanic eruptions, nature has been kind to St. Vincent's 110,000 inhabitants. Bananas, coconuts, cacao, eddoes and yams all flourish on the "Breadfruit Island", so called because it was the first in the Caribbean to be planted with the bumpy-skinned vegetable brought to the islands from the South Pacific by the legendary Captain Bligh. The island has long been the world's greatest producer of arrowroot, a starch used in the preparation of baby food and cooking sauces. Sea-island cotton, one of

ST. VINCENT AND THE GRENADINES

N

Fancy

Soufrière

Rabacca Dry River

Richmond Beach

Richmond Peak
3523 ft.

ST. VINCENT

Petit Bordel Bay

Georgetown

(Mesopotamia)

Barrouallie

Marriaqua Valley

Colonaire Bay

Layou Bay

Kingstown

Peruvian Vale

Fort Charlotte
Arnos Vale Airport

Argyle

Young Island

THE GRENADINES

Bequia

Port Elizabeth

Mustique

Petit Mustique

ATLANTIC

Petit Canouan

Canouan

Mayreau

Tobago Cays

Union

Palm

Petit St. Vincent

0     10     20 km

0          10          20 miles

the softest fibres in the world, is still exported, although not in great quantity anymore.

## Historical Highlights

Like neighbouring islands, St. Vincent passed back and forth between the British and French, especially during the troubled 18th century when the whole Caribbean area was in turmoil. European supremacy was never absolute, for the Caribs fought with all their mettle and ferocity. Several times the French seemed to make progress with the tribe, and they attempted to teach them the elements of trade.

Towards the end of the 17th century, a boatload of African slaves was shipwrecked on the Atlantic shore. The Caribs welcomed them, and soon a new race of Black Caribs sprang up. (A few descendants of this mixing still inhabit St. Vincent today.)

But the Caribs remained basically hostile, and they often rose against the white men. In 1748 St. Vincent was declared a kind of no-man's-land by both British and French, who were at their wit's end with belligerent Indians. The island was officially ceded to the English in 1763, only to be taken by the French in 1779, then made British in 1783.

In 1795 islanders sided with the French against British colonizers in the Brigands' War—murdering, burning down houses and setting fire to cane fields. However British reinforcements proved stronger in the end, and in 1796 the British overpowered the opposition and dispatched over 5,000 troublemakers to Honduras.

Emancipation took place peacefully under British rule. A few years later indentured labourers were brought from Portugal and India to work the cane fields. To this day, traces of their cultures remain, though many of the original 19th-century workers returned to their homelands.

In 1969, St. Vincent became a British Associated State, achieving complete independence ten years later. Recently there has been unrest in St. Vincent's Grenadines, notably on Union Island, but the government has been able to keep the peace. Tourism has been undisturbed, though the occasional curfew can curb late-night activities.

*On market Saturdays, the people of Kingstown stock up on sturdy baskets, breadfruit and bananas.*

## Kingstown

There are arcades to spare in St. Vincent's unassuming capital, many of them left over from French Colonial times. The **harbour,** in sight of Mount Andrew and Dorsetshire Hill, is always alive with schooners, fishing boats and the business of loading island produce.

Kingstown's food **market** ranks among the best in the Caribbean, especially on weekend mornings, but the small city (population 25,000) offers little else in the way of tourist attractions.

Shops are situated near the seaport and market. In Grenville Street, towards the other end of town, you'll see a trio of churches: St. George's Anglican Cathedral, the Methodist Church and **St. Mary's Roman Catholic Church.** This last, a fanciful pot-pourri of Romanesque, Gothic and Renaissance styles, would delight any storybook illustrator. There are towers, crosses and fretwork all over, and courtyards are situated in odd places. Surprisingly, it's a recent construction, built in the 1930s by Benedictine monks from Trinidad.

Learn all about Caribbean plant life at the **Botanic Gardens,** just below the Governor's Residence. The gardens, said to be the oldest in the Western hemisphere, were founded in 1765. Self-appointed guides are more than willing to point out the highlights of the well-maintained site.

**Fort Charlotte,** just west of Kingstown, merits a visit for the view, if nothing else. Take a panoramic look at the capital, harbour and nearby Grenadines through the handy telescope erected at the top of the fort's 636 feet. The fort was built by the British as a defence against the French and named after the wife of King George III. Three of the original cannon are still in place, and the lookout point is used for monitoring ships.

The fort saw no military action, unless you count the murder of a Royal Scots sentry in 1824 by a member of his own regiment. The austere former barracks building now serves as a museum displaying colourful contemporary paintings by William Linze Prescott. The canvases depict some rather lurid scenes from St. Vincent's history.

The Women's Prison, a short distance downhill, looks out on one of the loveliest views in the world. For more stunning views of Kingstown and the harbour, climb east of the city up to **Dorsetshire Hill,** taking the twisting road from Sion Hill near Arnos Vale airport.

## Along the Caribbean Coast

From Kingstown, drive northwest via the Leeward Highway, the name for the narrow road that twists its way along the coast. As you travel northwards, you come upon one stunning sea view after another, and in between there are small towns like QUESTELLES, a community of primitive houses and neat churches. Just before

*A Caribbean Eden: St. Vincent's Botanic Gardens, founded in 1765.*

the small fishing village of LAYOU BAY, stop to admire **Indian petroglyphs,** stone carvings estimated to be at least 1,400 years old. From here, you can make a short detour inland to the picturesque and jungle-like VERMONT district.

A further 3 miles brings you to **Barrouallié,** one of the last whaling villages in this part of the world. These days a catch is rare, and you're not very likely to see a whale.

The road winds north again through little settlements with amusing English or French names. One Gallic-named bay, for example, is called PETIT BORDEL which means either "Little Brothel" or "Little Mess" in French. Some 30 miles from Kingstown, the road comes to an abrupt end near Richmond Beach, a deserted place ideal for a picnic or swim.

## Towards the Atlantic

Drive south-east along the coast past the Kingstown airport. You travel through the town's main residential and hotel district into suburbs where English-style mowed lawns surround large villas. You soon see **Young Island,** just 200 yards offshore. Although the island has been developed as a luxury resort, non-residents are able to cross over on the hotel boat to enjoy a drink or a meal and explore the grounds. For a small charge, you'll be permitted to use the pool or the small beach. Fort Duvernette, on an adjacent islet reputed to have figured in battles with the Caribs, is now the scene of torch-lit barbecue suppers.

Head back to the mainland and continue north past a yachting centre and a few good beaches. You enter farming country, including land broken up into small plots planted with peanuts, yams, potatoes, cassava and corn. Coconuts are another important crop in this fertile area.

The road, now known as the Windward Highway, parallels the shimmering volcanic black-sand beaches of the Atlantic coast. Stop at **Mount Pleasant** for an impressive view of the pounding surf. But beware: winds, rough water and sharp rocks make swimming in the Atlantic dangerous. Farther along, the green ARGYLE district—a former plantation still planted with arrowroot, coconuts and other crops—extends up to PERUVIAN VALE.

From here to the village of GEORGETOWN, you drive through more impressive Atlantic scenery. From George-town, a poor road that can only be traversed by jeep leads to RABACCA DRY RIVER, a region marked by former volcanic activity, and FANCY, a village situated at the northern tip of the island.

Alternatively, you can head inland to the **Mesopotamia** district, otherwise known as the Marriaqua Valley, one of the island's most picturesque regions. **Belvedere Point** looks out over this agricultural area.

*A snorkel and mask open up an exotic new world under water.*

Green and richly cultivated fields climb neatly terraced hillsides interspersed with pretty villages. Every inch is planted with peanuts, nutmeg, bananas and plantain.

There are dizzying drops down to rushing streams and rivers like the Yambou. Every day seems to be laundry day, and you see many women (men, too) beating clothes against stones in the clear rivers. The people are attractive, but touchy and proud. You'll probably annoy them if you brandish a camera. To return to Kingstown, take the Vigie Highway, the most direct road.

## La Soufrière

This full day's excursion for the very hardy is best attempted on an organized tour. Starting out early in the morning, you travel by car, switching to a land-rover which carries you over dirt roads to the vicinity of the 4,048-foot crater. The climb up takes 2 to 3 hours—through hot (and sometimes rainy) jungle territory, but with plenty of rewarding plant and bird life to be seen.

*A vivid dash of blue makes a bold human contrast on St. Vincent.*

Soufrière has been well-chronicled in recent history as a fairly violent volcano. The biggest explosion occurred in May, 1902, when at least 2,000 inhabitants were killed. Later in this century, a scenic crater lake was formed, and in 1970 and 1971, minor explosions gave birth to an island in the centre of the crater. But all this island. Though walking is arduous, the excursion shouldn't be dangerous, as the volcano is constantly being monitored and warnings are issued when violent activity is foreseen.

## Grenadine Highlights

At least 100 islands (600 if you count all the rocky outcrops) extend for some 35 miles between St. Vincent and Grenada, spraying down like the beads on a necklace. The main islands in St. Vincent's domain—Bequia, Mustique, Canouan, Mayreau, the Tobago Cays, Union, Palm and Petit St. Vincent—are considered the ultimate Caribbean paradise for fishermen, snorkellers and yachtsmen*. For city dwellers seeking solitude, tranquillity and extraordinary beauty, there are few island groups that compare with the sparsely inhabited Grenadines, peopled by some 18,000 inhabitants.

**Bequia** (BECK-way or BECK-wee). This small but civilized gem about 9 miles from St. Vincent has no airport, so you have to make the 1- to 2-hour journey by boat. You dock in Port Elizabeth's colourful **Admiralty Bay,**

scenery was destroyed by the gas-and-ash eruption of April 1979. It was not a major disaster, however, since nobody was hurt. Problems came mainly from the big layer of ash, thrown up almost 5 miles high, which settled down on agricultural growth and temporarily blanketed even the best hotel lobbies.

If you climb to the top of the crater today, you'll find a mass of whitish-grey hot ash in place of the one-time lake and

---

* A description of islands administered by Grenada appears on p. 58.

which is jam-packed with yachts and looks like a festive regatta all year round. On the beach, fishermen mend their nets and make hand-built boats, an important local industry. You may even be lucky enough to attend a boat launching, a merry, but rowdy celebration that sometimes lasts all night.

Make a visit to the Tourist Board—the small building on the left as you face **Port Elizabeth** from the beach—to orientate yourself and plan your stay. The main island sights can be reached in a hired taxi. Allow half a day to see them all: OLD FORT affords a good view of Admiralty Bay; **Paget Farm** is a quaint whaling village; VISTA POINT offers views of St. Vincent and other islands; FRIENDSHIP BAY has a small hotel, reached over rutted roads; and MOON HOLE, a troglodytic residential development, has literally been carved from the cliffs. Note that the road to **Princess Margaret Bay** (noted for its beautiful coral reef, excellent snorkelling and tranquillity) is so poor that it is best reached by boat.

**Mustique** (mus-TEEK). The blinding white sand beaches and undulating green scenery have made Mustique a favourite hideaway of Princess Margaret and many other celebrities. But for all its publicity, Mustique looks more like a desert island than a gathering-place for the jet-set.

You may go no farther than one of the sandy beaches or the minuscule port of **Britannia Bay,** a famous yachtsmen's and sailors' haunt—unless you stay at the **Cotton House,** the island's single hotel, a restored 18th-century landmark. This exceedingly luxurious establishment bears all the earmarks of rustic elegance, with louvered windows, Spanish silver screens and a fountain of scallop shells.

**Canouan.** Blessed with beaches that are exceptional, even by Caribbean standards, the island is currently being developed as a discreet resort.

**Union** and surrounding islands. You can fly to the beautifully mountainous Union, the southernmost of St. Vincent's Grenadines. There are a few small hotels and many beaches. On the resort-hotel islands of **Petit St Vincent** and **Palm Island,** life is casual but chic. You can hire small boats for day excursions to uninhabited islands like MAYREAU and the TOBAGO CAYS, where you'll picnic and swim in splendid isolation.

50

# St. Vincent/Grenadines Briefing

**Airport.** Arnos Vale Airport on St. Vincent accommodates small planes only. The airport has a tourist information counter, bank, bar and restaurant and small duty-free shop. It is 3–5 miles from the major hotels, or 3 miles to the centre of Kingstown. You could take the colourfully painted bus, but a taxi is faster. The airport charges a small departure tax. For information on getting to the Grenadines, see INTER-ISLAND TRAVEL, pp. 120–21.

**Currency.** Eastern Caribbean dollar (EC$), 100 cents = EC$1. You might hear the old term "Bee Wee dollar" (for British West Indies). Notes: EC$ 1, 5, 20 and 100. Coins: 1, 2, 5, 10, 25, 50 cents and EC$1.

**Electric current.** 220/240 volts, 50 cycle AC. U.S. appliances will need a converter.

**Emergencies.** Dial 99 for police or fire, 61185 for ambulance.

**Hospitals.** Kingstown has a government hospital, tel. 61185, and a privately owned one, tel. 71747. There are also hospitals in Georgetown and on Bequia (Grenadines).

**Hours.** *General business and shopping hours:* Monday to Friday 8 a.m. to noon and 1 to 4 p.m., Saturday 8 a.m. to noon. *Banks:* Monday to Thursday 8 a.m. to noon or 1 p.m., Friday 8 a.m. to noon or 1 p.m. and 2 or 3 to 5 p.m.

**Newspapers.** The *Star* and the *Vincentian* are published weekly.

**Public Holidays.** New Year's Day (January 1), Discovery Day (January 22), Good Friday and Easter Monday (movable), May Day (first Monday in May), Caribbean Community Day (first Monday in July), Carnival (first Monday and Tuesday in July), Emancipation Day (first Monday in August), Statehood Day (last Monday in October), Christmas Day and Boxing Day (December 25 and 26).

## Tourist Information Offices

*St. Vincent:* St. Vincent Tourist Board, Halifax Street, P.O. Box 834, Kingstown, tel. 61224

*U.K.:* Eastern Caribbean Tourist Association, 15B Thayer Street, London W1M 5LD, tel. (01) 486-9119

*U.S.A.:* Caribbean Tourism Association, 20 East 46th Street, New York, NY 10017, tel. (212) 682-0435

# Grenada

This volcanic island possesses the same kind of rugged beauty that graces St. Vincent and St. Lucia—with one notable difference. Nutmeg, introduced in 1843, has become the island's principal export. In fact, Grenada produces about 25 per cent of the world's supply. It may be the power of suggestion, but the breezes wafting over the "Isle of Spice" do seem aromatic.

There is no shortage of sophisticated hotels and luxurious residential developments on Grenada, and the sandy beaches, including the famed Grand Anse, literally run on for miles. If you come to Grenada by air, the drive from the airport 18 miles across the island to the capital, St. George's, provides as scenic a tour as you'll find anywhere. You travel through tropical rain forests, past gorges of stunning beauty, and within hailing distance of a dormant volcano. At the end of the trip is St. George's harbour and the sea—a sun-washed spectacle that incites painters to pick up brush and palette.

*The Isle of Spice boasts bananas and a wealth of other fruits.*

## Historical Highlights

Columbus sailed past the northern tip of Grenada, now the small port of Levera Bay, which he called Concepción. Spanish sailors later named the island after their native Granada. The French then turned this into Grenada, though the British had the last word, pronouncing it gre-NAY-da.

Columbus was lucky not to have seen the island's beauties too closely, because the Caribs were particularly fierce on Grenada. Early attempts by both British and French to subdue them failed. In 1650, the French under Du Parquet and Le Comte purchased land from the Caribs in exchange for knives and hatchets, brandy and glass beads. But the Caribs weren't pacified for long, and they soon rebelled against the occupiers. A campaign of extermination was carried out. When defeat was certain, the last small group of

**GRENADA**

fighting Caribs jumped to their death from a northern cliff, now known as Morne du Sauteurs or Leapers' Hill.

By 1705 the French had established a settlement at Fort George, overlooking St. George's harbour. But by 1762, the British moved in again, ousting the French, who retaliated and regained the island in 1779. This uneasy French rule lasted until the 1783 Treaty of Versailles definitively established British rule, bringing to a close the French-English tug-of-war.

The century closed with a slave uprising in which the Lieutenant-Governor and many British citizens were killed. However, after emancipation, the island settled down. It was formally declared a Crown Colony in 1877.

After the establishment of an elected legislature in 1924, Grenada gradually moved towards independence. The island was made a British Associated State in 1967, and became fully independent in 1974. A coup d'état in the spring of 1979 brought several years of unrest, culminating in military intervention by the United States government in October 1983. But to the casual visitor, there are no signs of strife.

## St. George's

Start your visit to the capital with a stop for maps and information at the Grenada tourist office, situated on the east side of the **Carenage.** The picturesque inner harbour preserves some attractive 18th-century warehouses, and the lively restaurants and bars in the waterfront area make favourite meeting-places for tourists and yachtsmen alike. From here, walk east a short distance to the **Botanical Gardens and**

**Zoo,** majestically heralded by a clump of royal palms. The gardens bloom with an array of tropical flowers, and you may sight some brilliantly plumed Caribbean birds.

Make your way back to the waterside. You'll see Fort George high on its hill, an impressive structure erected by the French in 1725. The building now serves as police headquarters and cannot be visited. Sendall Tunnel leads from the Carenage to the **Outer Harbour** and quayside **Melville Street,** a lively shopping centre. Walk one street inland along Granby Street, a crossroad lined with cosy shops, to **Market Square,** site of a wonderful, typically West Indian open-air market. Among the wares for sale in the area are all manner of straw goods,

*The Carenage, St. George's inner harbour: one of the most striking sights in the Southern Caribbean.*

carvings and paintings. The profusion of local spices—from the commonplace nutmeg to ginger root, cinnamon and coriander—will find favour with the most demanding gourmet.

Follow Granby Street to the crossroads with Church Street, named after the churches that line it. Pay particular attention to **St. Andrew's Presbyterian Church,** distinguished by a square clock tower that is something of a town symbol. Return to Granby and take its continuation (Lucas Street) all the way up to Richmond Hill and **Fort Frederick,** a magnificent lookout point. Construction was begun by the French in 1779, but it was the British who applied the finishing touches in 1783.

The residence of the Governor General nearby is known as "Government House", but the building is distinguished only for the views it affords.

## Points South

Head south from St. George's along the **Royal Drive,** named in honour of Queen Elizabeth, who was escorted this way on a tour of the island (allow two hours for the complete circuit). You'll probably want to stop on the MORNE JALOUX RIDGE to admire views fit for a queen.

The road winds down through green hills past neat, small settlements and farming country to WESTERHALL POINT, a landscaped residential area which grows greener and wilder towards the point that projects into the sea. As you reach POINT JEUDY, you'll see black volcanic rock rearing out of an active sea.

Continue to WOBURN, a quiet little fishing village, then on to LANCE AUX EPINES and PRICKLY POINT, site of a few hotels and a bathing beach. From here, the road travels through the cane fields of WOODLANDS with its sugar factory. Along the route there are good views of pretty little coves. At POINT SALINE an international airport is under construction.

Caribbean and Atlantic water come together here, and the black, volcanic sands pounded by the Atlantic give way to the white sandy beaches that stretch northwards up the Caribbean coast. One of them, **Grand Anse Beach,** has won renown for the silvery whiteness of its two-mile expanse. Some of Grenada's best hotels and restaurants are situated along it, but the beach itself never seems crowded and it has a desert-island air.

## Spice Country

Good organized tours from St. George's visit the spice plantations in the northern part of the island. Many people hire a car and undertake the journey on their own, though the poor roads make driving difficult. The route follows the west coast, with bays and headlands of uncommon beauty.

Along the way you pass GRAND MAL BAY, HALIFAX HARBOUR and some of the prettiest fishing villages of Grenada. Hidden among the red roofs of GOUYAVE (officially Charlotte Town) is a **factory** where spices are sorted and dried in preparation for

*Two miles of paradise regained: the silvery beach of Grand Anse.*

shipping all over the world. Chief among factory products are nutmeg and the mace made from its filament. The heady scents will no doubt tempt you to buy small jars or baskets of fresh spices to take home. To see spices growing on a traditional plantation, head inland a short distance to **Dougaldston Estate,** a centre for the cultivation of nutmeg and cacao.

Other highlights of the north include SAUTEURS and nearby MORNE DU SAUTEURS

**57**

(Leapers' Hill), the rocks from which the last of the hostile Caribs plummeted to death in 1650, rather than surrender to the French. The cliff is not as spectacular as one would imagine, but the rocks about 40 feet below look sufficiently sinister.

Just east lies LEVERA BAY and its inviting beach, a good place to swim on calm days. Columbus reputedly saw this very place as he passed the little offshore islands of LEVERA, GREEN and SANDY.

Continue down the eastern coast to **Grenville,** just south of the airport. Grenada's second-largest town seems more like a casual village than a city, with a lively market and its own spice factory. Turn inland here to return to St. George's, taking the spectacular road with hairpin turns that serves the airport. The many spice plantations in the area can be identified by the red cacao nuts drying in the sun, and you may see boys with cutlasses harvesting the bountiful crops of coconuts, plantains and nutmeg.

The road passes **Grand Etang,** an extinct volcano 1,800 feet high that cradles a beautiful blue lake of 13 acres. Formerly off-bounds, the region is open to explora-

tion now, and camping is permitted. You may also want to go (perhaps with a picnic and bathing suit) to **Concorde Falls,** a series of three cascades in a setting of spice and banana trees, accessible from the Western Main Road.

## Grenada's Grenadines

Both Carriacou (23 miles north-east of Grenada) and Petit Martinique (3 miles east of Carriacou) come under the jurisdiction of Grenada. Regular boat services operate here, and there are air connections from several islands to Carriacou. Ample, if fairly simple, hotel accommodation is available only on Carriacou.

**Carriacou** (pronounced CARRY-coo) has won the acclaim of yachtsmen for its friendly hospitality, which becomes positively raucous during boat launchings or the August Regatta. The French originally settled the island, planting sugar cane and building roads all over Carriacou's 13 square miles. But the British coveted the place and finally wrested it from the French in the 18th century.

*Nutmeg and mace are the spice of life in Gouyave: a local factory worker oversees production.*

# Grenada/Grenadines Briefing

**Airport.** Pearls Airport accommodates small planes only (no jets). There is regular air service from Barbados and Trinidad. This is a small airport with a café and duty-free shop. Pearls is at the opposite end of Grenada from St. George's (the capital) and the main hotels. A pretty 18-mile taxi ride will get you to your destination. Bus travel is impractical. A small departure tax is charged when leaving the island. Grenada is planning a big, modern airport at Point Saline, convenient to hotel and residential areas. For information on getting to Carriacou and Petit Martinique, see INTER-ISLAND TRAVEL, pp. 120–21.

**Currency.** Eastern Caribbean dollar (EC$), 100 cents = EC$1. Also referred to as "Bee Wee" (British West Indian) currency. Notes: EC$ 1, 5, 20 and 100. Coins: 1, 2, 5, 10, 25, 50 cents and EC$1.

**Electric current.** 220/240 volts, 50 cycle AC.

**Emergencies.** Dial 2244 for police, 2112 for fire, 2113 for ambulance.

**Hospitals.** General Hospital, St. George's, tel. 2051. You'll also find hospitals in St. Andrew's parish, tel. 7251, and on Carriacou.

**Hours.** *General business and shopping:* Monday to Friday 8 a.m. to 4 p.m. with a lunch break (about 11.45 a.m. to 1 p.m.). Thursday and Saturday 8 a.m. to noon only. *Banking hours:* Monday to Thursday 8 a.m. to noon, Friday 8 a.m. to noon and 2.30 to 5 p.m.

**Newspapers.** The *West Indian* (daily except Monday and Friday) and the *Torchlight* (three times a week).

**Public Holidays.** New Year's Day (January 1), Independence Day (February 7), Grenada Revolution (March 13), Good Friday and Easter Monday (movable), Labour Day (May 1), Whit Monday (movable), Corpus Christi (movable), Emancipation Day (first Monday in August), Christmas Day and Boxing Day (December 25 and 26).

## Tourist Information Offices

*Grenada:* Grenada Tourist Board, P.O. Box 293, The Carenage, St. George's, tel. 2001/2279

*Canada:* Grenada Consulate of Trade and Tourism, 143 Yonge Street, Suite 101, Toronto, Ont. M5C 1W7, tel. (416) 368-1332

*U.K.:* Grenada Tourist Board, c/o Grenada High Commission, 1 Collingham Gardens, Earls Court, London SW5, tel. (01) 373-7808

*U.S.A.:* Grenada Mission & Information Office, 141 East 44th Street, Suite 905, New York, NY 10017, tel. (212) 599-0301

Today, the legacy of France lives on in the persistence of French place names and the patois spoken by the islanders. Most of the inhabitants are descendants of African slaves, or emigrants from Scotland. Those whose names begin in "Mc" are usually employed in boat building.

The sleepy "big" town, **Hillsborough,** wakes up at Regatta time. The rest of the year the island is left to sailors and snorkellers. People travel here just for a look at the area's spectacular coral reefs, the habitat of "tree-oysters" which attach themselves to mangrove roots.

**Petit Martinique** can count no more than 600 inhabitants, who are mostly of French descent, though English is spoken. Islanders are known both for their maritime prowess and their boat building. Smuggling is said to be an important occupation, too. Sailors may take refuge in the harbour, but there is no tourist accommodation here.

Other fairly deserted and beautiful islands popular with the yachting set include ILE DE RONDE, KICK 'EM JENNY (supposedly a corruption of *Quai qui gêne* or "Annoying Reef"), CONFERENCE and GREEN BIRD.

# Trinidad and Tobago

Opposites *do* attract, especially when they're neighbours, as are Trinidad and Tobago, the southernmost of the Southern Caribbean islands. They're only 20 miles apart; they have one government and speak as one nation. The combined population is 1,350,000 of which Tobago represents some 50,000. Their union is something of a marriage of convenience, for the two islands were joined artificially in 1889, after Tobago's sugar industry collapsed and the island needed Trinidad's support.

These islands are as different as oil and water. Life in business-orientated Trinidad revolves around Port-of-Spain, the sophisticated capital. Blessed with the inestimable asset of oil, the bigger island is being courted by energy-seeking nations. Tobago proves a more restful and seductive place, with an abundance of natural beauty and pleasant resorts to attract holiday-makers. The two islands complement one another, and it is interesting to see them one after the other.

For details on travel between the sister islands, see Briefing, page 81, and INTER-ISLAND TRAVEL, page 120.

**61**

# Trinidad

Take an island with rich natural resources and lush scenery, people it with a vast selection of races and faiths, add plenty of steel-band music—and you have a thumbnail sketch of Trinidad.

The island covers a large area of 1,864 square miles, about 50 by 35 miles. It probably broke away from Venezuela in a distant geological age, a theory given credence by the striking similarities in rock formation, flora and fauna between Trinidad and Venezuela, which lies some 7 miles to the south.

## Historical Highlights

Columbus himself named Trinidad in 1498—both for the Holy Trinity and the triple mountain peaks he could see from his ship. Spain founded a rather half-hearted colony on the island in 1532, but Trinidad remained poor and largely undeveloped. Sir Walter Raleigh chanced by in 1595 and burned down most of the newly founded Spanish town of San José. He also happened upon Pitch Lake—a marsh that provided excellent caulking for his ships. In fact, Pitch Lake still supplies asphalt for roads the world over.

During the next hundred years, the number of Spanish colonizers dwindled to about 30. Then new settlers arrived, bringing with them black African slaves to work extensive coffee, sugar cane, cacao and cotton plantations. New blood and energy flowed into the island in response to a 1783 Spanish royal proclamation calling upon Roman Catholics of all nationalities to settle and work on Trinidad. This encouraged the ethnic diversity that still characterizes the island.

Spanish Trinidad was captured by the British in 1797, although Spain did not concede the change in ownership until 1802. Thus the island became a British colony, loyal to the Crown.

When slavery was abolished in 1833, the former slaves went inland to set up small farms. Thousands of indentured labourers were recruited to replace them, resulting in an influx of Hindus, Moslems and Parsis from India and the Far East. Today they make up over one-third of the island's population.

The collapse of the sugar market in 1884 bankrupted neighbouring Tobago, and the island was joined to Trinidad in 1889. Early this century, oil was discovered on Trinidad,

While World War I did not affect the islands greatly, the United States built bases on Trinidad during World War II to safeguard the Caribbean.

As a Crown Colony, Trinidad had been given a small measure of self-rule, but further independence was requested by both Trinidad and Tobago. On August 31, 1962, Trinidad-Tobago was officially declared independent. The two islands became a republic in 1976, while continuing as a parliamentary democracy. There are 15 members of parliament from Trinidad and three from Tobago. The chief executive is the President.

Friction arises between Trinidad and Tobago, since Tobago feels it has little voice in government and no real power in the delegation of money for improvements. Many Tobagonians would prefer independence, but the fact is Trinidad has the oil and the money.

TRINIDAD

## Port-of-Spain

Lush green hills surround the capital of Trinidad-Tobago, and the multi-racial population lives in everything from shacks to imposing colonial palaces. The architecture embraces a variety of styles from neo-Gothic to glossy contemporary, and the restaurants vary from French or Indian to fast food. Port-of-Spain is dotted with parks of all shapes and sizes, which Trinidadians like to compare to London's. However, the similarity between England and Trinidad ends with cricket, and you'll never doubt for a moment that you're in the tropics.

Begin your exploration of the city on **Frederick Street,** a main artery lined with shops that runs from north to south between Queen's Park Savannah (see p. 67) and the port. As you walk from the Savannah, you pass the modern Town Hall at the corner of Knox Street. Not far away on the opposite side, the friendly staff of the Tourist Board occupy offices at No. 56.

Next you come to **Woodford Square,** a large green space. Take a right at Knox Street and continue along the square to **Red House,** a stately colonial building (1906) that is now the seat of government. The elaborate bi-coloured stone building nearby on Edward Street is neither a fortress nor a mosque, but rather the central Police Headquarters. Now cross back to Frederick Street along the south side of Woodford Square, fronted by the neo-Gothic **Anglican Cathedral.** Peep inside at its beautifully carved mahogany altar and choir stalls.

(You may want to make a detour to the Jama Masjid Mosque, which lies directly east along Queen Street, a crossroad of Frederick. Note that the mosque is situated in the East Dry River district, an unsavoury part of town that should not be entered without a guide).

As you near the harbour, Frederick Street is closed to traffic, and hawkers selling

*The Red House: stately seat of government in Port-of-Spain.* **65**

souvenirs congregate in the area, urging passersby to part with their money. The crowds and the colourful scene extend to **Independence Square,** a wide double thoroughfare thronged with tourists seeking bargains in the big duty-free shops. The street, fortuitously laid out by the Spanish as a military parade ground, serves admirably as an assembly point for participants in Carnival parades, *the* event of the Trinidad year.

The banks on almost every corner symbolize Trinidad's financial importance. A statue in memory of Andrew Cipriani, a World War I hero and former mayor, stands in the strip of park dividing the parallel streets; another a short distance away is dedicated to Columbus.

The **Roman Catholic Cathedral** is situated here, too. This simple stone structure with two bell towers and a wood-vaulted interior dates from

QUEEN'S ROYAL COLLEGE,
PRESIDENT'S PALACE, ZOO,
BOTANIC GARDENS

Queen's Park
Savannah

Alcazar Rd

Marli St.

Queen's Park West

Queen's Park East

Industry La.

Erthig

Jerningham

Suffolk

Tragarete Road

Alberto Street

Rosalino Street

Alfredo St.

Elizabeth St.

Robert St.

Gray St.

Rust St.

Herbert St.

Maraval Rd.

Warner

Queen's Avenue

Park

Ave.

Albion

National Museum
Art Gallery

Keate Street

Frederick Street

Charlotte Street

Henry

General Hospital

Darce

Ariapita Avenue

Luis Street

Carlos St.

Murray

Picton Street

Cipriani Blvd.

Woodford Street

Tranquillity Melville Lane

Stanmore

Gordon Street

Abercromby St.

Pembroke Street

St. Vincent

Belmont Circu

Wrightson Road

Alfredo St.

Carlos St.

Fitt Street

Kitchener St.

Robert St.

Bulla St.

Victoria

New Street

Edward Street

Oxford Street

Cornelio

Baden Powell

Ariapita Avenue

French Street

Methuen St.

Scotland St.

McDonald St.

Tragarete Road

Lapeyrouse Cemetery

St. Fraser

Krew St.

Philip

Park

Borde

Richmond Street

Edward Street

St. Vincent Street

Frederick Street

Henry Street

Charlotte Street

Observatory

Basil Rd.

Belle

N

Dock Area
(Port Authority)

Wrightson Road

Flament St.

Scott Bushe St.

Stone St.

Victoria Square

Duke Street

Charles Street

Town Hall

Knox St.

Red House

Woodford Square

Duke Street

Abercromby St.

Prince Street

i Tourist Board

Central Market

George Street

Nelson Street

0   200 m
0   200 yard

Dock Road

Sackville St.

London St.

Ajax St.

Queen St.

Charles Street

Anglican Cathedral

Chacon St.

Queen Street

St. Vincent Street

Rom Cath Cath

King's Wharf

Gulf of Paria

**PORT-OF-SPAIN**

Independence      Square

1844. Local people keep in voice year-round for Carnival, and services and choir rehearsals are often enlivened by a definite calypso beat.

From Independence Square you might go down to the waterfront, where tourist ships dock, and the Central Market in the Beetham Highway, a lively display of West Indian produce early in the morning.

## Queen's Park Savannah

This magnificent park, complete with race course, playing fields and plenty of food stands, occupies some 200 acres. Start your visit on the south side at the **National Museum and Art Gallery** on the corner of Frederick and Keate streets. Two Spanish cannon commemorating the British capture of Trinidad in 1797 and a big anchor supposedly lost by Columbus' fleet lure visitors inside.

To the right of the entrance stands a puncheon, one of the big barrels used in the manufacture of Angostura Bitters, a concoction invented as a cure for stomach upset in 1824 in Venezuela. Later the manufacturing plant was moved to Trinidad. Many of the exhibits are disappointing (minerals and woebegone stuffed spe-

cimens of local mammals), but persevere to see the exhibition of gaudy Carnival floats and costumes—insects, snakes, dragons and devils with enough net, sequins and feathers to make a cabaret artist jealous. Interesting, too, is a display of snake-bite cures. Paintings by local artists are sometimes on view, many excellent, some of them offered for sale at reasonable prices.

Head north along Maraval Road, the site of Queen's Royal College, a British legacy. The exterior of this boys' school is painted a colourful red and yellow. Continue past an extraordinary collection of old **mansions,** including the residences of the Anglican Bishop (blue and cream) and Catholic Archbishop (Spanish style). In between stands Roodal's House, decorated in a frothy Creole style that belies its local description of "French Second Empire".

Farther along you come to Whitehall, a graceful Moorish-style structure that serves as the Prime Minister's office. Don't miss Stollmeyer Castle, a white elephant of a house that belonged to a German family. This Rhenish, turreted stone affair would have suited the Wicked Witch of the West, or maybe even Dracula. But

*The cream of Trinidad society once lived in the old mansions that line Maraval Road; this one sports tall gables, fretwork and a shady veranda.*

somebody must love it, as it's been bought by a local family.

The quiet little zoo on the northern side of the Savannah contains chimpanzees and colourful birds with bright feathers, as well as a rather mournful lion (who looks as if he's dying of boredom) and some restless ocelots.

The **Botanic Gardens** next door prove more interesting, especially if you hire a guide. The 70-acre gardens were founded in 1818 by one of Trinidad's governors, Sir Ralph Woodford. Vandals have taken most of the plaques from the trees, but the guides will be glad to explain everything—from frangipani and sausage trees to the raw beef tree, which seems to bleed when you cut into the bark. There's also a peepul (bo) tree, the type under which Buddha achieved enlightenment. Adjoining the gardens is the President's Palace, formerly the Governor-General's residence, a Caribbean version of the neo-Renaissance.

## Outskirts of Town

The view of town from **Fort George** merits the bumpy ride uphill over a narrow, potholed road. The small house at the top of the fort overlooks the whole of Paria Bay, taking in the Trinidad Regimental Headquarters, Carrera Island (a work prison) and Leper's Island way off to the right. On a clear day, you can see all the way to Venezuela from this 1,100-foot vantage point.

More sweeping views can be enjoyed from the chapel dedicated to Our Lady of Laventille, 3 miles from town in the **Laventille Hills.** Spanish-built Fort Chacon (1784) is visible to the north and Fort Picton (1800), English-built, to the south.

You can reach the **Caroni Bird Sanctuary,** about 7 miles south of Port-of-Spain, by road or boat. Tour companies organize relaxing afternoon excursions by boat, very pleasant except for the hard seats (cushions are not provided). You travel along the Wayama River past endless mangrove trees, their tangle of long roots alive with tiny crabs and oysters.

Magnificent blue and white heron and other birds nest in the sanctuary, but the climax of the tour comes at sunset. Hundreds of scarlet ibis, like wispy clouds of flame, fill the sky with their bright-red feathers. When the birds settle at last on the mangroves, they transform them into Christmas trees heavy with ornament.

## Island Sights

You can drive yourself around the island, but it is more enjoyable to hire a car and driver for sightseeing, whether for a morning, an afternoon or a full day. Certain group excursions prove less expensive than car hire; ask at your hotel or the Tourist Board.

Swim in a Tarzan and Jane setting at **Blue Basin,** a hibiscus-edged pool fed by a waterfall. This idyllic spot, about 10 miles north-west of Port-of-Spain, is reached via the DIEGO MARTIN VALLEY and RIVER ESTATE, a cacao plantation. You have to walk a half-mile from the car park, but the tropical splendour of the site **69**

will richly reward you for your trouble.

A trip to **Maracas Beach,** one of the most popular swimming areas on the island and the best near the capital, makes another pleasant outing. Drive uphill past the Trinidad Country Club and Moka Golf Course to the North Coast Road, or Skyline Drive. There are panoramic views from the hilly area called THE SADDLE. Ask your driver to point out highlights of Trinidad vegetation: cacao plants, variegated hibiscus and teak, nutmeg and wild cotton silk trees. During the Christmas season, you'll see big candle-shaped blossoms on the towering piper tree, called a life plant because it oozes red sap when cut.

You soon cross the foothills of the Northern Range, which afford a view of the sea as far as Tobago. From here, the road runs downhill to Maracas Beach. Swimming is easy, though life guards are on duty in case of trouble. There are changing rooms, and snacks and drinks are available. A bus service operates from Port-of-Spain, but the schedule is irregular. If you dislike crowds, avoid the beach at weekends.

You could also visit the little town of **Chaguanas** (about a 45-minute drive south-east of Port-of-Spain) in the morning when the food market is in full swing. Here you can see and sample some of the West Indies' most exotic culinary specialties. Try the spicy Indian pastries—fiery but not harmful if your digestion is strong. Every sort of island staple is on sale, from the ugly gilbaca fish and fresh shrimps to dasheen, cassava root and goats' heads.

One of Trinidad's prime attractions, the **Asa Wright Nature Centre,** lies about an hour's drive east of Port-of-Spain, beyond Piarco Airport. The estate was originally built by German settlers, but the property changed hands and names many times before it was acquired by a state-owned scientific foundation. Tourists are welcome to join the bird-watchers, entomologists and botanists with special scholarly interests, who assemble here to study the flora and fauna of Trinidad. Many people come just to see the oilbird or guacharo, a rare species that inhabits caves in the grounds.

*A footpath meanders through Trinidad's tropical rain forest.*

*Hauling in the catch is the big event of the day on Trinidad; mangroves shade a quiet beach.*

More guacharos (and diablotins, too) can be seen at the nearby **Aripo Caves.** An array of stalagmites and stalactites add to the splendour of this little-frequented spot for the adventurous, a few miles north-east of ARIMA in the Aripo Road. In the distance rise two spectacular mountains, El Cerro del Aripo (3,085 ft.) and Chaguaramas (2,817 ft.). A visit to the caves can only be recommended to the hardy, since you must walk 2½ miles to reach them.

You have to be interested in asphalt to make the three hour journey by car to **Pitch Lake,** spoken of as one of the wonders of the world. Trinidadians claim that its 300-foot depths provide much of the world's road surfacing—something to think about as you drive along Fifth Avenue or creep around Piccadilly Circus.

The vast, grey "lake" has changed little since its discovery by Sir Walter Raleigh at the end of the 16th century. The surface is generally hard, but it oozes in places and could suck you in like quicksand, so take care in walking around.

Set aside a full day to explore the **east coast** of Trinidad, a beautiful but little-visited region planted with extensive coconut groves. From Port-of-Spain you pass through the scenic interior towns of VALENCIA and SANGRE, reaching the coast at **Cocos Bay,** named in honour of the coconut palms. Swimming is pleasant, and you may even bump into a strange species of fish, the "four-eyed" anableps. Another sandy beach shaded with a multitude of coconut palms lies farther south at MAYARO BAY.

# Tobago

Trinidad's neighbour has been christened "Robinson Crusoe's Island" for no good reason, except that it looks like a place where Defoe's hero might have been stranded. Nearly all of Tobago's 26 by 7 miles provides perfect scenery and relaxation. The island is unspoiled, but like every paradise in a natural state, there are a few drawbacks. You may encounter the occasional water shortage, and a casual attitude and easygoing way of life rarely produce quick service.

The Tobagonians couldn't be more different from the people of Trinidad. Most citizens are descendants of black slaves, and there is nothing like the heterogeneous mix of the larger island. People on Tobago are basically kind and helpful, though they complain constantly about the government in Trinidad, the laziness of their fellow Tobagonians, and so on.

There may be inconveniences for the tourist on this rustic island, but you'll forget all about them as you sip an exquisitely scented rum punch or swim in the turquoise sea.

## Historical Highlights

Tobago takes its name from the tobacco plant, or from the Spanish word for the natives' pipes. Spain was so busy colonizing Trinidad that Tobago was left to itself for at least a hundred years. Then early in the 17th century, the English attempted to settle the island; but disease and Carib raids decimated the inhabitants.

TOBAGO

For the next hundred years or so, Tobago's history was stormy, and the island changed hands between Dutch, French and English dozens of times—as regularly as the ball is knocked about in a game of tennis. The Dutch invaded in 1658, then English privateers took over (1666), followed the next year by the French, and so on. After the island was declared neutral territory in 1748, French-English rivalry grew even more intense.

Between battles, life went on. Slaves were imported and plantations started. By 1770, when the island numbered some 3,000 Africans and only 200 whites, the first slave uprising had taken place. From 1781 the French held sway, but the British regained control in 1793. The Treaty of Amiens returned Tobago to France in 1802, but not for long. The British were back again in 1803, landing at Arnos Vale Bay. They were aided by a slave called George Winchester, who later won his freedom and became Tobago's first black businessman.

With it all, Tobago became a great sugar-producing colony, giving rise to the local expression "rich as a Tobago planter". When emancipation took place in 1834, slave labour became paid labour, after a fashion. In spite of a disastrous hurricane in 1847, sugar, rum and cotton production boomed. Rich little Tobago was made a Crown Colony in 1877. But prosperity came to an abrupt end in 1884 when the sugar market collapsed. As a result of the economic disaster, Tobago was made a ward of Trinidad five years later.

Along with Trinidad, Tobago gained independence in 1962. Although construction and development has brought change to the island, Tobago has kept a great deal of its primitive aspect and charm.

## Scarborough

Tobago's capital, a sleepy little town of 10,000 on the southwest coast, lies about 10 miles from the airport and a good 30 minutes from most resort hotels. Scarborough looks like a shantytown when public works are underway, as is often the case, but it's a friendly place. To help visitors, the Tourist Board has established headquarters in an old colonial building right in the centre of town.

**Fort King George** (completed 1779), the principal sight, stands above Scarborough. From its 450-foot elevation you can see Bacolet, a prosperous residential area, and Trinidad. Both the island's hospital and the former prison are situated downhill from the fort. The once formidable prison was the scene of a revolt in 1801 that ended in the sentencing to death of 39 prisoners. According to legend, the governor was loath to carry out so many executions, but to save face, he ordered that one body be strung up over and over again.

The fort bears witness to French-English rivalry for the island, and a plaque commemorates every change of fortune: France 1781, Great Britain 1793, etc. A bronze cannon from the George III period remains in place, and there are plenty of exotic plants to admire, especially in the peaceful garden of a ruined church on the site.

## South-west of Scarborough

Head south-west in the direction of the airport. You pass excellent sandy beaches with hardly anyone in sight, even in the peak season. This is an inviting place to snorkel and bathe in the surf.

For a nominal admission, you can enjoy the spectacular stretch of fine sand at **Pigeon Point,** near the swampy BON ACCORD LAGOON. There are changing rooms, cabanas and a simple bar-restaurant.

**Buccoo Reef,** an extensive coral reef that is one of Tobago's main attractions, lies about a mile offshore from Pigeon Point and Bon Accord Lagoon. Glass-bottom boats reveal the wonders of the warm tropical sea, and you'll marvel at the Queen triggerfish, blue tang, yellowtail, snapper and other beauties of the deep. For a clear view underwater, be sure to make the trip on a fair day at low tide. Swimmers can use the boat's snorkel equipment, and there are rubber-soled sandals for protection against coral cuts and sea urchins.

You may want to make use of the beach facilities at the **Mount Irvine Bay Hotel,** a luxury installation just north or its 18-hole golf course, one of the best in the Caribbean. Non-residents are welcome.

## Towards the Caribbean

A scenic road leads north-west of Scarborough, passing **Fort William,** a well-maintained red-brick building that serves as the official residence of the Trinidad-Tobago President. Farther along you'll see a plantation Great House called The Whim. Not long afterwards you arrive at the town

*The lively charms of Tobago contrast with the rusted remains of an old abandoned sugar mill.*

of PLYMOUTH on the coast. A tombstone in Plymouth was inscribed in 1793 with a puzzling epitaph in memory of Betty Stivens: "She was a mother without knowing it, and a wife, without letting her husband know, except by her kind indulgences to him". Islanders translate this as a classic love story between a master and his black mistress. She was the mother of the man's children, and was honoured by marriage to him

77

only after her death, when the master also recognized the children.

The **Great Courland Bay Monument,** situated on a point, commands a striking view of the sea, and there is good swimming from the beach below. The monument was erected in memory of "the enterprising and industrious Courlanders from faraway Batavia on the Baltic shores, who lived in this area..." The cannon nearby mark the site of Fort James, built in 1768.

Continue north-east along the coast to the **Arnos Vale Hotel,** a former sugar plantation. Some drivers refuse to attempt the rough country road to the property. A disused sugar mill fitted out with a formidable crushing wheel made in Glasgow in 1857 stands on the grounds. Some of the guest rooms are situated in the gracious plantation house, and an 18th-century clavichord lends its elegance to the sitting room.

The event of the day at Arnos Vale is **bird-watching** at tea-time. This pleasant activity will never tire you, for while you sit and sip your tea, the birds flock to you: the yellow-breasted bananaquit, Tobago blue tanager, ruby topaz hummingbird and handsome, **78** orange-breasted king of the woods or mot-mot. In just one afternoon, you can become an amateur ornithologist.

Not far away at GRAFTON ESTATE, you can also watch the birds. For either place, go around 4 p.m., the best time to see and feed the birds.

From Arnos Vale poor roads travel north-east to CHARLOTTEVILLE, a fishing town, but a good local driver will have no trouble negotiating the turns. Scenic highlights include precipitous views of headlands and the sea, alternating with picturesque huts on stilts serving as bars, stores or post offices. There are good swimming beaches at CASTARA BAY, ENGLISHMAN'S BAY and PARLATUVIER, a fishing village with pastel houses.

You may want to make a detour inland to the **Tobago Forest Reserve,** where trails invite long hikes. Ask for good maps and information at the Tourist Board in Scarborough. In the Charlottesville region are the sandy beach at MAN O'WAR BAY and Pigeon Peak, the island's highest point at nearly 2,000 feet. A road links the town to Speyside on the Atlantic.

*Bananaquits pose obligingly for birdwatchers in garden setting.*

## Atlantic Sights

Take the scenic road that travels east from Scarborough along the wild Atlantic coast. The drive to Speyside takes 2 or 3 hours. Tiny villages like MESOPOTAMIA, GOLDS-BOROUGH and ROXBOROUGH line the way. You may want to stop for a swim at one of the bays just before Roxborough: PRINCE'S, QUEEN'S or KING'S.

Continue to SPEYSIDE, a colourful beach settlement. From here you can see tiny

*Gingerbread house in full bloom rivals colourful garden on Tobago.*

Goat Island and **Little Toba-go,** a 450-acre bird sanctuary, also called Bird-of-Paradise Island. To see the birds at close range, take a boat to the island from Speyside, a one-hour trip. In addition to the native birds that congregate here, there are dozens of other species, including gilt-plumed birds-of-paradise.

# Trinidad-Tobago Briefing

**Airports.** Trinidad's Piarco International Airport is 18 miles south of Port-of-Spain. There are duty-free shops, a tourist office which will handle your mail and change money, a hairdressers, snack bar and car-hire desks. Porters are not in evidence. Taxis are always available (the ride is about 45 minutes). The airport levies a small departure tax. The flight from Piarco to Crown Point Airport on Tobago takes about 25 minutes; the Tobago airport has limited facilities.

**Currency.** Trinidad-Tobago dollar (TT$), 100 cents = TT$1. Issued in 1, 5, 10, 20 and 100-dollar notes and coins of 1, 5, 10, 25 and 50 cents.

**Electric current.** 115 or 230 volts, 60 cycle AC.

**Emergencies.** Dial 999 for police, 990 for ambulance.

**Hospitals.** *Trinidad:* General Hospital, 164 Charlotte Street, Port-of-Spain, tel. 62-32951. *Tobago:* Scarborough General, tel. 639-2500.

**Hours.** *General business and shopping hours:* Monday to Thursday 8 a.m. to 4 or 4.30 p.m., Friday 8 a.m. to 6 p.m., Saturday 8 a.m. to noon. *Banking hours:* Monday to Thursday 9 a.m. to 2 p.m., Friday 9 a.m. to 1 p.m. and 3 to 5 p.m.

**Newspapers.** Two dailies, the *Guardian* and the *Express;* and the *Evening News* (weeknights and Saturdays).

**Public Holidays.** New Year's Day (January 1), Eid-ul-Fitr (Moslem festival, movable), Carnival (unofficial, Monday and Tuesday preceding Ash Wednesday), Good Friday and Easter Monday (movable), Whit Monday (movable), Corpus Christi (movable), Labour Day (June 19), Discovery Day (first Monday in August), Independence Day (August 31), Republic Day (September 24), Divali (Hindu festival, movable), Christmas and Boxing Day (December 25 and 26).

## Trinidad & Tobago Tourist Boards

*Trinidad:* 56 Frederick Street, Port-of-Spain, tel. 62-31142

*Tobago:* Piggott Street, Scarborough

*Canada:* York Centre, 145 King Street West, Toronto M5H 1J8, tel. (416) 367-0390

*U.K.:* 20 Lower Regent Street, London SW1Y 4PH, tel. (01) 839-7155

*U.S.A.:* Suite 712, 400 Madison Avenue, New York, NY 10017, tel. (212) 838-7750/7751

# What to Do

## Sports

The Southern Caribbean islands, famed haunts of beachcombers and yachtsmen, offer an array of sports possibilities as dazzling as the sand, sea and sunshine. You can jog along the firm, sandy beaches; swim, sunbathe and sail; or search the coral reefs for beautiful underwater views. If you observe the usual sun and heat precautions and take care to develop a suntan gradually, you'll return home relaxed and healthy.

There's an island for every sport. Resorts on Barbados, Grenada, St. Vincent and, to a lesser extent, Tobago, hire out equipment and provide instructors. Parasailing and water-skiing are tops on Barbados and St. Lucia. In the Grenadines, however, there are fewer sports facilities, but many glorious beaches. While Trinidad has a great deal to offer the tourist, the best hotels are situated inland, and the atmosphere is not really holiday-orientated in the sense of beaches and water sports.

Day cruises to areas good for snorkelling operate on most islands.

*Water sports are tops on beaches such as this: Young Island, just 200 yards off the St. Vincent shore.*

# Water Sports

## Beaches and Swimming

Miles of sandy beaches, usually golden or silvery-white, rim the islands. There are some volcanic black-sand beaches on St. Vincent and Grenada, but these prove more popular with sightseers than swimmers. The islands' beaches are open to everyone, but you may be expected to pay for a mat or a chair at beaches developed by resort hotels.

Some swimming areas are roped off for good reason: there may be a dangerous undertow, sharp-cutting coral or sea urchins there. Make sure of swimming conditions and the availability of a life-guard before taking small children or learners into the water. The windy Atlantic beaches are washed by a wild and woolly surf dangerous for all but very good swimmers. There are big waves, and experts can surf in some places.

Outstanding beaches are to be found along the St. James coast (Barbados); at Choc Bay, Vigie Beach and Marigot Beach (St. Lucia); Grand Anse Beach and Levera (Grenada); and Pigeon Point (Tobago). There are adequate beaches at the resort hotels near Kingstown (St. Vincent), but these **83**

### Underwater Wonderland

A host of exotic creatures inhabits the watery depths of the Caribbean. Common sights include elkhorn, finger and brain coral, which look exactly as their names imply. In addition, you may see fire and pillar coral, as well as sea fans. Take care not to step on the razor-sharp coral, and refrain from breaking off samples, a practice frowned upon by the authorities.

Fish are not at all shy about parading their gorgeous colours past snorkellers and divers. Look for the bright-blue-and-yellow Queen Angelfish, the orange-and-blue Honeytail Damselfish and striking Queen Triggerfish. The blue Ocean Surgeon has a neat "incision" marked in black on its gill, and the Sergeant-Major sports pretty blue, yellow and black stripes.

are far surpassed by the idyllic strands of the Grenadines, too numerous to list.

### Snorkelling

A passion with many island visitors, snorkelling is particularly good off Tobago (especially Buccoo Reef), Barbados, St. Vincent, Grenada and most of the Grenadines.

Good swimmers can explore on their own, and there are guided snorkel tours on many islands. Equipment is sold almost everywhere. Diving services and some hotels hire out masks and flippers; other hotels loan masks and flippers free of charge.

### Scuba Diving

You may not rival Jacques Cousteau at first, but lightweight diving equipment will enable you to see a whole new underwater world—from shipwrecks to strange and beautiful fish. There are diving centres on many islands and hotels often provide scuba (an acronym for Self-Contained Underwater Breathing Apparatus) facilities. A three-day introductory course, including classroom study, is usually compulsory for beginners.

## Other Water Sports

Many resort beaches hire out motorboats and drivers for water-skiing. Instruction is often available. Some of St. Lucia's major hotels include 15 minutes of water-skiing (and a half-hour of sailing) daily in the price of the room. Otherwise, you'll have to pay by the hour or day; prices vary considerably from island to island.

Windsurfing is becoming increasingly popular, and equip-

*Come on in, the water's lovely! Scuba diving is easy, fun and safe—after a few simple lessons.*

ment for this strenuous, demanding exercise in balance now exists at many resorts. Barbados specializes in parasailing, a thrilling extension of water-skiing. Towed by a motorboat, you take off from a floating launch wearing a harness fitted with a parachute. You soar into the air for a few minutes and land again on the launch. It's harmless fun for anyone in good health who likes heights.

## Deep-Sea Fishing

The best season for game fish runs from November to April. Depending on where you are, you can catch blue or white marlin, barracuda, kingfish, dolphin and wahoo. Up to six fishermen can charter a small boat, and local fishermen, especially around St. Vincent and the Grenadines, often permit enthusiasts to join them in a hard day's work. You have to set out at about 3 a.m., but you'll certainly catch plenty of edible varieties this way.

## Boats and Sailing

Hiring small sailboats (called sunfish), motorboats, catamarans or other vessels is a simple matter in the Southern Caribbean, and there is often no other way to reach deserted islands, coves and nearby reefs. You can arrange to charter a yacht on St. Lucia, St. Vincent or Grenada, the islands with the best facilities and harbours. Depending on the terms of hire, the price may include food, drink and crew's wages. Many yacht charters allow you to "cruise and learn" with sailing instruction from the crew. Ask at the various tourist offices for information.

## Sports Ashore

### Tennis
There is no shortage of courts on the islands. Many hotels have built their own; others have unlimited access to courts nearby. Non-residents can often play on private hotel courts on payment of a hire charge. There are several public courts on Trinidad and Barbados; most of them are just as good as the hotel courts, for half the price.

### Golf
Clubs on the major islands readily admit visitors for a small fee. You can generally hire clubs and the services of a caddy. Try the fine 18-hole course at Sandy Lane (Barbados) or the Barbados Golf and Country Club at Christ Church.

In good British tradition, Trinidad and Tobago boast eight golf courses between them, including Moka, Brighton and Point-à-Pierre. Tobago's 18-hole Mount Irvine course, the site of professional tournaments, is celebrated as one of the best.

On St. Lucia, there are pleasant and scenic nine-hole courses at Cap Estate Golf Club and Hotel La Toc. St. Vincent's nine-hole Aquaduct course is situated in an attractive tropical setting about half an hour by car from Kingstown. The Woodlands on Grenada offers views of the Atlantic and the Caribbean with every putt.

### Horse Riding
Canter along scenic trails on Barbados and St. Lucia, the only islands in the Southern Caribbean where riding facilities are available. Stables in the Barbados parishes of St. Michael's and St. Thomas are readily accessible to resort hotels. There are many scenic trails, especially around Sam Lord's Castle. St. Lucia's rid-

ing is from Cap Estate in the north-west to Pigeon Island and other places of great natural beauty.

## Spectator Sports

Enthusiasm for cricket has never waned in this former British enclave, especially on Barbados, where the season runs from June to January. Matches are played at the Kingston Oval.

Football (soccer) has its devotees, and on Barbados and Trinidad polo attracts large crowds. In addition, there are horse races held two to four times yearly on Barbados, Trinidad and Tobago.

## Hiking

There are countless places to explore in the jungles and hills of Trinidad, Tobago, St. Lucia, Grenada and St. Vincent. In fact, you can only reach St. Vincent's Soufrière volcano by foot (see p. 48). It's a good idea to hire a competent guide, except perhaps on Barbados, where the gentle terrain makes for ease of walking. Be sure to bring sturdy shoes.

*A British legacy, cricket remains a favourite game on the islands; here a match in Port-of-Spain.*

# Shopping

Several islands offer outstanding duty-free bargains in luxury goods such as jewellery and china, but shops in Barbados probably offer the widest range of items and the best service. Look for establishments labelled "in-bond" or "duty-free". Tax-free purchases are sealed and delivered to you after you've gone through customs at the airport or dock. You can also send

*Caribbean beaches are good for shopping, too. You can make your purchases from a stall on the sands.*

tax-free goods by mail. but the postage may be prohibitively expensive.

Every island also produces a good deal of craft work, though specialities vary from place to place. Hand-crafted articles are available in regular shops or on the beach, where prices are cheaper and a little bargaining is part of the fun.

Works of art by native artists include colourful primitive painting and attractive African-style woodcarving and sculpture. Ask tourist offices or hotel staff for the addresses of the best galleries and workshops.

Wherever you go, you'll find a selection of small souvenirs, from elaborate, costumed dolls in ruffled dresses to straw articles. Postage stamps make another worthy memento of the islands, since each nation produces its own beautiful designs.

Here is what to look out for on the various islands:

## Barbados

Shops generally open on weekdays from 8 a.m. to 4 p.m., Saturdays 8 a.m. to noon. There are smart boutiques all over the island, especially in or near the resort hotels. The main shopping street in Bridgetown is Broad Street.

Duty-free buys include transistor radios, cameras and Swiss watches, as well as a selection of china, glass and crystal. You'll also find tobacco, cigarettes, perfume and spirits, with Barbados rum a bestseller. For last-minute shoppers, the Barbados airport has some nice, small duty-free shops.

Clothing for men and women can be an interesting item, especially cashmeres, cottons, silks and accessories. A few tailors will stitch up suits for men in a few days. Women's sports clothes are good, whether sold in boutiques or on the beaches.

You can buy excellent beach-wear where you bathe from colourful little racks set up daily (except Sundays) by local seamstresses. Men and women both like the brightly printed unisex overblouses. And most women want at least one airy sarong, which can be tied in various ways. There are also comfortable long caftans and pretty sundresses. Most styles come in miniature for children.

Handicraft items typical of Barbados include reed or straw place mats, sisal or straw bags and baskets, various articles (jewellery in particular) made from seashells and coral; ceramics are also available. In **89** some shops, good batik is sold—for a price. Beware of washing the cloth, which isn't always colour-fast.

## St. Lucia

Main shops open weekdays and Saturday, except Wednesday, 8 a.m. to 12.30 p.m. and 1.30 p.m. to 4 p.m., Wednesday 8 a.m. to 12 noon. A couple of shops in Castries sell very nice print and batik sportswear for women, and there are boutiques selling clothes and souvenirs in the better hotels. You can carry home the heady scent of tropical flowers in the form of locally blended perfume.

Dolls, pretty stamps and shell necklaces are sold everywhere, and you'll also see beaded jewellery, small carved wooden objects, and the usual local straw and sisal articles: bags, baskets, hats and rugs.

## St. Vincent

Shops open Monday to Saturday, 8 a.m. to 12 noon, weekdays only, 1 to 4 p.m. Apart from the usual duty-free spirits and perfume, there is also a small selection of crystal and china. Local crafts items are similar to those of St. Lucia: straw and sisal goods, carved wooden objects and coral necklaces. Some of the batik

sold here is of very high quality.

On all of the populated Grenadines, you'll find small souvenirs and sportswear. Particularly useful on these islands are the green palmfrond sun hats, woven for you on the beach.

## Grenada

Shopping hours are 8 to 11.45 a.m. and 1 to 4 p.m. Monday to Friday. The most obvious buys on the Spice Island are spice baskets woven of straw or palm fronds and filled with ginger, cinnamon, nutmeg and so on. Near the market in the centre of St. George's, you'll find all sorts of hand-crafted goods, from hand-blown glass to straw hats, bags and mats. There are also many shops selling china, spirits and other duty-free goods. Certain shops and hotel boutiques sell very attractive batik caftans and overblouses, as well as resort wear in African or Liberty cottons.

Look, too, for tortoise-shell objects and jewellery, china and ceramics. A few shops stock excellent British woollens and cashmeres—if you can face choosing winter clothing in the tropics. There are also a couple of galleries selling the best of island art.

## Trinidad and Tobago

Shopping hours are 8 a.m. to 4 p.m. Monday to Thursday; 8 a.m. to 6 p.m. Friday and 8 a.m. to noon Saturday. Port-of-Spain's best shops are in Frederick Street, Independence Square, and in or near luxury hotels.

Duty-free (in-bond) goods include a wide selection of cameras, binoculars, watches, perfumes and spirits. There are also some cashmere, shetland and silk items, though not in great abundance. Larger shops stock china, crystal, glass and silver.

A few shops specializing in men's custom tailoring can make a suit in a few days' time. In general, resort and town clothing for women isn't up to the standard of the other islands, though Indian silks, cotton shirts and caftans could be good buys, and typical loose shirts can be picked up in the street for a song.

Other popular buys include a vast array of silver and gold filigree Indian-style jewellery. Many women visitors pick up a chiselled gold or silver bangle bracelet or two, to be in

*A young craftsman learns the time-honoured methods of his trade.* **91**

tune with the Trinidadian women.

There are many local handicrafts for sale, such as carved Indian or African-style wooden or ivory statues and figurines. Woven straw and fibre objects range from little boxes to attractive fish-shaped place mats, shoulder bags and carryalls. The sisal and straw furniture is good-looking, but you must be able to transport it home. The selection of costumed dolls reflects Trinidad in all its variegated glory—with rich sari-clad Hindu dolls, ruffled dancing girls and fanciful Carnival performers.

If you like island music, buy your own "pan" or steel drum and learn to play it. And, of course, to evoke the total sound, you can buy excellent recordings of calypso, steelband and Carnival tunes.

For the best Trinidadian painting and sculpture, go to the Port-of-Spain Museum, where works of art are sometimes sold, or ask your hotel or the tourist board for the names of reputable galleries.

Tobago is not really a place to shop, though you can find a few interesting local souvenirs like shells, tortoise objects and dolls, as well as a small selection of luxury goods and sportswear in the larger hotels.

## Entertainment

### Carnival

All the Southern Caribbean islands celebrate Carnival, but none of them can match Trinidad's eye-opening display, staged on a scale equal to Rio

*A lithe dancer takes off in a burst of butterfly garb at Port-of-Spain's Carnival, a dazzling spectacle.*

de Janeiro's. Carnival was originally a French custom, brought to the islands by French immigrants in the 18th century. At first the festival was a rather dignified expression of jollity, with masked balls, *fêtes champêtres* and carriage promenades. But things began to swing after Emancipation in 1834, when freed slaves took part.

They brought with them *canboulay* (from *cannes brûlées*)—a celebration associated

## Steelband...

This unmistakable sound is known all over the world—beautiful music from oil drums. It all started in Trinidad in 1937, when a ragtag group led by "Lord Humbugger" marched into Port-of-Spain during a Carnival parade playing "pans" to an enraptured crowd. Soon budding musicians all over the island were shaping and tuning steel oil drums.

At first there was disapproval of the jumbled jazz being produced in the shanty towns. World War II interrupted activity, but post-war bands came out in force. Players hailed from all walks of life, though most of them were seeking a creative outlet from the poverty of the slums.

Steelband music was refined more and more, and today a "pan tuner" commands a good deal of respect. He tempers the metal with heat, then hammers it with a sledge hammer, taking care to make indentations that will produce the best steelband sounds when struck with mallets.

Steelband is now a musical way of life all over the Caribbean, and the compositions and range of tones can be astonishing. From the latest popular hits to unique renditions of Mozart or Bach, every band takes pride in its own special repertoire.

## ...and Calypso

Trinidadians also take credit for inventing this special form of music with its catchy rhythm and witty (sometimes suggestive) lyrics. Calypso evolved over a period of more than 200 years, though songs weren't written in English until the turn of the century.

The word "calypso" probably derives from "cariso", a song-and-dance act performed by women between men's duelling acts during Carnival, though the word may have its origin in "kaiso", a West African dance-chorus. The music combines slave songs and African rhythms with French, Spanish and Irish musical traditions, not to mention some Chinese and Indian elements.

Harry Belafonte popularized calypso in songs like "Matilda" and "Little Bird". There are many types of calypso, including songs for work and play, shango or popular religious songs and songs of revolt. What you hear today is often a sophisticated mix of political and personal observation, not always easy to understand if you don't know **94** the local dialects and expressions.

with the old plantation custom of burning off cane stalks left in the fields after harvest. New rhythms and music of Spanish and African origin were introduced, as well as unconventional musical instruments made of bamboo, gourds and bottles.

Fun was fun, but the situation got out of hand on Trinidad when hoodlums joined the ranks and *canboulay* turned into torch-lit riots with stick-fighting in 1881. In the 1890s, however, Carnival made a comeback, and competitions for masquerading groups of bands wearing thematic costumes were organized.

*In the Southern Caribbean, nightlife is never boring. Wearing glitter, satin and smiles, lavishly costumed dancers whirl the night away.*

Today, tension and excitement build up in the weeks preceding Carnival. Big bands with hundreds and even thousands of participants start rehearsing in earnest just after the New Year, and the public can buy tickets to rehearsals. Carnival itself is limited to a mere 43 hours, from 5 a.m. Monday (*J'ouvert, jour ouvert* or opening day) to midnight Shrove Tuesday. Everyone celebrates in wild abandon, literally collapsing as Ash Wednesday dawns.

Port-of-Spain's Carnival opens with "Ole Mas", the crowning of the King of Carnival, and the first big bands shuffle into Independence Square, during "Lil Mas" Monday afternoon, already dancing to the music. By Monday evening, the festivities are in full swing. More costumed bands parade, and spectators pack the streets to join in, carried away body and soul by the compelling rhythms. Plenty of rum is imbibed, and the atmosphere grows euphoric.

Prizes are awarded for music and costumes, but the awed visitor is hardly aware of the fine points. The final day of parades (Mardi Gras) takes place at the Savannah. It's a mind-boggling spectacle of light, sound and colour, with costumes that make Hollywood extravaganzas look tame.

You might want to avoid the hysteria of the actual celebration and participate in the warm-up during the week or two before Carnival instead. In any case, reserve your hotel and parade seats at least a year ahead, if possible. Remember that pickpockets find Carnival ideal for practising their trade. Leave valuable items in your hotel safe, and take a minimum of money to the parades.

## Nightlife

Music swells up in the islands, and there's dancing in the dark, the moonlight, the streets. Most nightlife centres around the hotels, which can provide excellent entertainment, from calypso and fire-eaters, to slightly more elaborate shows. But the atmosphere is usually rather sedate, with dancing to live music. On some islands, there are small cinemas, including a few drive-in theatres. Symphony, opera and ballet hardly exist, but no one seems to care.

Top pop groups perform on Barbados and Trinidad. Your hotel will know what's on and where. Many islands have a weekly entertainment guide. When you go to a hotel other than your own, you're expected to have at least a drink if there's no entry fee. Sometimes the price of admission includes the first drink.

There are also discos, *boîtes*, low dives and big outdoor clubs providing floor-shows and musicians to keep you dancing. Barbados offers the biggest choice of nightlife of all the islands in this guide. Groups of calypso dancers, limbo artists and fire-eaters migrate from hotel to hotel. Anyone who is reasonably dressed—usually men don't even need a tie—can gain admission anywhere.

There aren't many dives that tourists dare or care to frequent, but they do exist, and can be amusing, especially those around the dock area of Port-of-Spain. Barbados has an infamous tawdry section just north-east of Bridgetown. Go with extreme caution (women with escorts).

The only casino in the Southern Caribbean is situated on St. Vincent, about a 30-minute drive from Kingstown. The atmosphere is casual, and there are no special dress requirements. You can play roulette, black-jack and slot machines, and the low minimum bets must be the most reasonable in the world.

# Dining and Drinks

Picture a fresh catch of fish and shellfish, a multi-coloured choice of glistening and exotic fruits and vegetables and an aura of spice. This is the essence of Caribbean cooking at its best. Despite the prevalence of hamburgers and steaks on some menus, many restaurants make an effort to serve typical Caribbean dishes—the result of a happy marriage of fresh products and time-honoured recipes evolved from the culinary traditions of Africa, Spain, France, India and England.

Throughout the Southern Caribbean, lunch is served from about 12 to 2 p.m. and dinner from 7 to 10 p.m. In addition to hotel restaurants, there is a wide range of eating houses. You can sample highly flavoured East Indian curry dishes or specialities straight from Peking (especially in Trinidad), as well as exotic island fare. Most menus are written in English, though you may come across some mysterious local terms. However, waiters and waitresses are helpful in describing unfamiliar dishes.

## Breakfast

The first meal of the day may be simple continental, hearty American-style or an elaborate buffet featuring salt-fish and corn fritters. But whatever else you're served, the joy of breakfast is fresh tropical juices and fruits, especially grapefruit, juicy orange pawpaws (papayas), pineapple, mangoes and watermelon.

*Fresh fruit is always available.*

## For Starters

Before you tackle the menu with its tempting array of specialities, relax with an aperitif or cocktail and crisp plantain chips deep-fried in coconut oil. Plantain—similar in appearance to a green banana but much firmer and not nearly as sweet—makes a good introduction to island tastes.

Among the wide variety of first courses are *pastelles*, plantain or banana leaves stuffed with a corn meal and savoury meat filling. *Accras*, lightly fried herbed codfish balls, can be served with a piquant sauce or (especially in Trinidad) with "floats"—puffy, fried yeast biscuits.

You may be able to try *tan-tan*, a Barbadian dish of marinated chicken livers cooked in brandy-flavoured batter. Trinidad's *bol-jol*, salt-cod served with pickled cucumber and lime, is available throughout the region.

The more familiar dishes include shrimp salad and fried scampi (particularly delicious on Trinidad and Tobago, but good everywhere), *prosciutto e melone* (Italian-style ham and melon), curried eggs and potato salad.

## Soups

The islanders have a gift for concocting delicious soups from local products. Most famous is Trinidad's *callaloo*, more like a full meal than a mere soup. It has become a standard Caribbean dish, though ingredients and spelling may vary from island to island. The basic recipe calls for dasheen leaves (similar to spinach), okra, onions, garlic, chicken stock, salt-pork or beef, coconut milk, crab meat and hot pepper seasoning to taste.

Here are some soups exotic enough for the most jaded palate: cream of breadfruit (hot or cold), avocado, cream of pumpkin or *christophene* (a local variety of squash). Highly spiced pigeon-pea soup is usually made with coconut milk and a little ham or salt-pork.

Black-bean soup is popular, and you can hardly go wrong with cream of crab, an aristocrat among soups on all the islands. There is also fish soup, **101**

called *bouillabaisse* on some islands. Jellied orange or lemon consommé is refreshing on hot days and light enough to please the diet-conscious gourmet.

## Fish and Seafood

Always ask for the catch of the day in the Caribbean. You'll be tempted by crab backs, crab shells stuffed with a spicy crab-meat filling, a speciality of Trinidad that is available on most islands. Shrimp is wonderful, whether deep-fried in batter, in a cream sauce, or grilled barbecue-style.

*Lambi*, chewy conch meat, appears on menus in the fishing villages of St. Lucia, St. Vincent and the Grenadines; it's served cold with lime, having been chopped and stewed beforehand. Conch is also used in pies and soups.

Spiny lobster can misleadingly be referred to as lobster in the Caribbean. It's also called crawfish, *langouste* and *langosta.* But whatever the name, this tasty crustacean is expensive and good, whether grilled and served with melted butter or cold with herb-flavoured mayonnaise.

Be sure to try flying fish, especially in Barbados: it's lightly fried and served with lime wedges and tartar sauce or cut into fingers and deep fried. The dolphin served in these parts has nothing to do with "Flipper". The small, white-fleshed tropical fish can be prepared many ways, usually fried or steamed and seasoned with herbs.

Coquilles of fish—shells filled with scallops or billfish—may be served temptingly *au gratin* in a wine-flavoured sauce with mushrooms. Red snapper, scallops, swordfish and kingfish are prepared in every imaginable way, from sautéed or fried to poached or baked. Sauces can be tangy, and many fish dishes are seasoned with curry spices.

## Meat Specialities

Meat is popular, though often imported. You'll find good steaks and other cuts of beef, as well as pork and lamb—prepared in all the usual ways with the chef's favourite sauce.

But there is one outstanding meat dish served in various forms all over the islands and especially on Trinidad and Barbados. This speciality, known as pepperpot, reputedly originated with the South American Indians. It's a succulent stew of pork and beef, perhaps even chicken, though the key ingredient in most recipes is casareep, a spicy mixture of grated cassava, cinnamon and brown sugar. Very different is *pelau* (or *pi'au*), a Trinidad speciality probably introduced by the Muslims. This rice-based dish combines fish or chicken, tomatoes, garlic, onions, and plenty of coconut milk, raisins and *garam masala* (curry spices).

If you're lucky enough to see *sancoche*, try it as a main dish. It's a "soup" of pork and pig's tail, with lots of beef and stock, cassava, yams, potatoes, chives, peppers, perhaps coconut milk. You'll probably agree that it's far too filling to qualify as a starter. Another soup in this same special category, pudding and souse, combines black pudding (blood sausage) and *souse*, lime-marinated ham hocks.

Chicken, duck, turkey and guinea fowl or *pintadeau* are served frequently in the islands. The meat can be stuffed and roasted or served in sauces. *Canard à l'orange* and curried chicken are both delicious. Goat and rabbit are prepared in a variety of interesting and tasty ways by local people, but you rarely see these meats on menus.

## Vegetables
Imaginative cooking does justice to the exotic offerings of Caribbean gardens. Plantains can be cooked as a savoury vegetable. Try warm plantain balls, called *foo-foo* in Trinidad and Barbados. Cucumbers are delicately sautéed, as is *christophene*, a kind of squash. This vegetable can also be cooked *au gratin* in cream sauce.

Both *dasheen* (the tuberous part) and breadfruit may be boiled, sautéed or fried. Dasheen leaves are used in *callaloo* soup, and breadfruit resembles squash in taste.

*Coo-coo* technically means a side dish, but this usually implies corn meal or semolina, cooked in various ways on the different islands. Barbados and Trinidad-Tobago cooks add okra to the corn meal, combining the ingredients in a mould and serving the dish as an accompaniment to meat.

## Snacks
There's never a problem if you're hungry between meals, but street-stands may not be the best place to eat if you have a delicate stomach. In Trinidad many stands sell apples (wash them first), plus Indian specialities like deep-fried *kachouris* (chick-pea fritters), *poulouris* (cakes of split-pea meal) and *sahinas* (fritters of ground split peas with saffron). **103**

Use the accompanying sauces with caution; they can be very potent.

Shops selling chips (French fries) vie with peanut vendors and pizza, corn fritter and meatball sellers. You can also fall back on fast-food, as the American chains are making inroads in the Caribbean.

**Desserts**
The wealth of fresh fruit provides a host of refreshing desserts. Mangoes, passion-fruit, grapefruit, bananas, pawpaws and pineapple are just a few of the possibilities. Fruit salads can be excellent, especially with a dash of liqueur or rum. *Crêpes flambées* may be filled with exotic fruits.

Bananas are served fresh, flambéed, fried and in bread or cakes. Soursop, a tangy fruit, is sometimes made into a good ice or a cold drink. Trinidadians with a sweet tooth like guava cheese, made by boiling the fruit down with sugar till it reaches a jellied consistency when cooled.

Gateaux or cakes range from sweet and custard-filled varieties to those made with excellent bitter chocolate. Fruit

**104**  *A mouth-watering dessert display.*

and liqueurs figure in many recipes. Dessert trolleys often display pies as well, especially a lime pie similar to that made on the Florida Keys, as well as the irresistible frozen lime pie.

Coconut is used liberally in cakes, puddings, cream-filled pies and tarts. And the English preference for trifle is well catered for, since the rich dessert calls for a liberal dose of rum. St. Vincent restaurants sometimes serve arrowroot custard, a kind of blancmange good with jams and fruits.

Ices and ice creams with a tropical taste include pineapple, coconut and ginger. If you tire of these, there are many varieties more, like mango, guava, lime—and even soursop for a change from the ordinary.

## Drinks

Non-alcoholic island favourites include fruit punch and coconut water from a freshly opened shell. *Sorrel*, a refreshing bright-red spicy drink made from a plant called rosella, is bottled on Trinidad. *Mauby*, another popular concoction, is made from roots and bark, with heavy lacings of cinnamon, clove and other spices. On Barbados you can sip the drink at a street stand, or take concentrate home to mix with sugar and water to your own taste.

While spirits and wine are available everywhere, the prices can be exorbitant. Many hotel restaurants serve table wines by the glass, for prices that go up and up. Beer is usually reasonably priced and good, as some islands brew their own—*Banks* (Barbados), *Carib* (Trinidad), *Heineken* (St. Lucia)—but the obvious drink is rum.

Each bartender has his own recipe for rum punch, which is often sprinkled liberally with nutmeg—an idea from Grenada. *Piña colada*, the perennial Caribbean treat, combines rum, coconut cream and pineapple juice, in a drink so rich it seems more like a sweet. Rum is added to *daiquiries*, swizzles and screwdrivers, too.

There are, in addition, fabulous inventions with names to match: "The Reverend's Downfall", a St. Lucia speciality, "Coco-Loco" and "El Dorado". If you're not careful, these sugary concoctions can give a mighty hangover.

If you want to drink water (and it's a good idea sometimes), water from the tap is safe on all the islands. Mineral water is considered an affectation, perhaps because it is very highly priced.

# How to Get There

Because of the complexity and variability of fares, you should ask the advice of an informed travel agent well before your departure.

## From North America

### BY AIR

**Barbados and Trinidad:** Regular non-stop service from Boston, Miami, New York, Montreal (Barbados only) and Toronto. Many connecting flights through Miami, San Juan or Toronto.

**St. Lucia:** Regular non-stop service from Boston, Miami, New York and Toronto.

**St. Vincent and Grenada:** You can reach St. Vincent and Grenada by changing aircraft in Barbados or Port of Spain (Trinidad). The main gateways are Miami, New York and San Juan.

**Package Tours and Charter Flights.** Sports programmes (golf, tennis, diving) are featured year-round. Many vacation packages are offered with or without car hire. If meals are not included in your package, the MAP (breakfast plus one other meal) plan is a money-saver.

### BY SEA

The Southern Caribbean islands are favourite stops on cruises originating in Florida or Puerto Rico.

## From Great Britain

### BY AIR

**Barbados:** Direct service from Heathrow on two major carriers. Caribbean Airways run flights from Gatwick.

**Trinidad:** Regular non-stop service from Heathrow; other flights stop in Antigua or/and Barbados.

**St. Lucia:** Regular non-stop service from Heathrow; other flights stop in Barbados.

**St. Vincent and Grenada:** Fly to Barbados, Trinidad or St. Lucia, then change to a local air carrier.

**Package Tours:** Package holidays are offered to one island or more in all price ranges.

## BY SEA

Although passenger lines no longer sail directly to the Caribbean from Great Britain, cruise operators now fly tourists out to the islands or Miami to join their ship.

### Between the Islands

Local air service between the islands is excellent. Daily flights link the six major islands mentioned in this book, and in some cases service is almost hourly. For further information, including boat services, see INTER-ISLAND TRAVEL, pp 120–21.

# When to Go

Southern Caribbean temperatures rarely reach unbearable levels, though humidity can be enervating in summer. Weather is best during the peak tourist season (December15–April 15), with lower temperatures and less rain, but prices are higher. The official hurricane season is from June 1 to November 30, but only an average of six hurricanes blow through the Caribbean each year.

Trinidad is crowded during Carnival (usually in February, sometimes early March), but the fun and spectacle are worth it.

Average monthly temperatures for Barbados:

| | | J | F | M | A | M | J | J | A | S | O | N | D |
|---|---|---|---|---|---|---|---|---|---|---|---|---|---|
| Temperature | °C | 25 | 24 | 25 | 25 | 26 | 27 | 26 | 26 | 26 | 26 | 26 | 25 |
| | °F | 77 | 75 | 77 | 77 | 79 | 81 | 79 | 79 | 79 | 79 | 79 | 77 |

# Planning Your Budget

To give you an idea of what to expect, here's a sampling of average prices. They can only be approximate, however, as inflation creeps relentlessly up.

**Airport departure tax:** From *Barbados* BD$12. *St. Vincent* EC$5 to Caribbean islands, EC$10 to other destinations. *Trinidad* TT$20 to all destinations. *St. Lucia* EC$6 and 12. *Grenada* EC$5.

**Buses:** *Barbados,* any one-way trip BD$0.75.

**Car hire:** *Barbados,* Mini-Moke US$55 per day, Toyota 1300 DX (automatic) US$75 per day. Add 8% tax. *St. Lucia,* Datsun 120 Y US$30 per day (including 40 free miles), Datsun 160 J (station wagon) US$33 per day (including 40 free miles).

**Cigarettes:** *Trinidad* local brands TT$1.50, imported $2–$3.50. *St. Vincent* local brands EC$1.20, imported $2–$3.

**Driving:** Temporary permit, *Barbados* BD$20. *St. Lucia* EC$15. *St. Vincent* EC$5. *Grenada* EC$5.

**Entertainment:** *Barbados* nightclub cover charge BD$15. *Trinidad* from TT$15. *Tobago* folklore show TT$10.

**Ferry:** Tourist ferry from *St. Vincent* to *Bequia (Grenadines)* US$5. Night ferry from *Trinidad* to *Tobago* TT$20.

**Hairdressers and barbers:** *Barbados* wash and blow-dry BD$20, cut $17, man's cut $15. *St. Lucia* shampoo and set from EC$15, man's cut from $10.

**Hotels:** High season, double room with bath, MAP. *Barbados* luxury from BD$300, average from $200. *St. Vincent* luxury from EC$275, average from $150.

**Motorcycle hire:** *Barbados* BD$30 per day, $140 per week.

**Taxis:** *Barbados* taxi from airport to central Bridgetown BD$20. *Trinidad* taxi from airport to Port-of-Spain TT$45, *Grenada* taxi from airport to any town or resort EC$50.

# BLUEPRINT for a Perfect Trip

## An A-Z Summary of Practical Information and Facts

A star (*) following an entry indicates that relevant prices are to be found on page 108.

Information particular to the individual islands is included in a handy Briefing section at the end of each chapter. Specific details are given on such subjects as airports, currency, emergency phone numbers, etc.

## Contents

Airports
Bicycle and Motorcycle Hire
Buses
Camping
Car Hire
Cigarettes, Cigars, Tobacco
Clothing
Communications (Post Offices, Telephones, Telegrams, Telex)
Complaints
Converter Charts
Crime and Theft
Customs and Entry Formalities
Driving
Embassies, Consulates, High Commissions
Guides
Hairdressers and Barbers
Health Precautions
Hitch-hiking

Hotels and Accommodation
Inter-Island Travel
Language
Laundry and Dry-cleaning
Lost Property
Maps
Medical Care
Money Matters (Currency, Banks, Credit Cards, Traveller's Cheques, Prices)
Pets
Photography
Police
Radio and TV
Religious Services
Taxis
Time Difference
Tipping
Toilets
Water

**A** **AIRPORTS.** Each of the major islands has an airport (St. Lucia has two) with varying facilities. See Briefing section under the various chapters. There are no porters in evidence at some airports. Take baggage you can manage yourself, if possible. Some hotels provide courtesy cars.

**Airport tax***. You have to pay a fee upon departure, the price varying from island to island. The tax is usually less for inter-island trips than for destinations outside the Caribbean.

**B** **BICYCLE and MOTORCYCLE HIRE***. Road conditions on most islands are not ideal for cycling or motorbike riding. Still, these can be rented in some places.

**Barbados:** For motorcycles or mopeds, enquire at:

A & T Motorcycle Rentals, Worthing, Christ Church

You must be 21 or over and a licensed driver for at least two years. A visitor's permit is required (available for a small fee).

Several companies rent bicycles, including:

Rydal Waters Guest House, Worthing, Christ Church
Chandler Hardware and Cycle Store, Bridgetown

You must be 21 and in possession of a valid driver's licence. A deposit is required. The cycle is insured, and personal accident insurance can be purchased for an extra fee.

**BUSES***. Buses are the only form of public transport on the islands, but they are not always comfortable or fast. Barbados has the most modern fleet (blue and grey). Pay as you enter at the rear of the bus.

Otherwise, all of the islands have brightly painted "shuttle" buses, some inscribed with colourful names. You hoist yourself up and take a seat on one of the small wooden benches. A conductor collects the fare, which is always reasonable, even for a long ride. Stops are indicated by small, circular signs marked "bus". These buses tend to be crowded.

**C** **CAMPING.** Camping is not officially encouraged on any of the islands. You can try to sleep on the beaches (not permitted on Barbados), but you may have to contend with insects, robbery or even worse. Check with the local tourist board first for advice on the best sites.

**CAR HIRE**★ (see also DRIVING). Both international and local car hire firms operate on the major islands. During the high (winter) season, it is advisable to reserve a car in advance, especially on Trinidad-Tobago and Barbados. Makes include Ford, Toyota, Datsun, Mazda and several others. The Mini-Moke, a kind of jeep, is popular all over, especially on Barbados.

Prices and conditions vary considerably. Mini-Mokes are sometimes cheaper to rent than other models, and require less petrol (gasoline). If payment isn't made by credit card, a deposit for the estimated rental charge, plus insurance fees, is often required.

You must be 25 years old to rent a car, and show a valid driver's licence (held for at least 2 years when renting from certain Trinidalian firms). On most islands (except Trinidad and Tobago, where you are required to have an International Driving Permit), drivers must purchase a visitor's driving permit from the local police station.

**CIGARETTES, CIGARS, TOBACCO**★. Most international cigarette brands are available throughout the Southern Caribbean. Some makes manufactured or packaged in the area are cheaper than imported brands. Cigarettes are sold at duty-free prices on all the islands, but they can be delivered to you only at the dock or airport. Several types of cigars and tobacco are available.

Smoking is allowed in most places, except on crowded buses and in certain taxis.

**CLOTHING.** It's easy to pack for a Caribbean holiday, since temperatures are high year-round. You'll need light clothing, preferably of cotton, which allows perspiration to evaporate more easily than synthetic fibres.

Informality is the keynote on the islands. Although clothing requirements vary from resort to resort, an elaborate wardrobe isn't necessary —even in the evening. Bustling Port-of-Spain is the only exception. Travellers will feel more comfortable in a lightweight suit or a cotton dress, especially for business appointments.

Beach attire is, of course, unsuitable in towns and public places. Topless and nude bathing are prohibited on public beaches.

**C**

Be sure to bring walking, jogging or tennis shoes, as well as rubber-soled footwear for beachcombing and snorkelling.

The islands are so warm that you hardly ever need much of a cover-up except, perhaps, in draughty air-conditioning. Take an umbrella for the warm rain that can fall between July and December. Hikers should take a light, waterproof parka, plus long trousers, long-sleeved shirts and a hat.

Clothes bought on the spot can be reasonable or even cheap in price, and tourists whose luggage has temporarily gone astray have been known to outfit themselves completely during a quick trip to town.

## COMMUNICATIONS

**Post Offices.** On the larger islands postal service is generally good. Main post office addresses and hours:

*Barbados:* Public Buildings, Bridgetown. Open 7.30 a.m. to 4.30 p.m. Monday to Friday, 8 a.m. to noon on Saturday.

*St. Lucia:* General Post Office, Bridge Street, Castries. Open 8.15 a.m. to noon and 1 to 3.30 p.m. Monday to Friday, 8.15 a.m. to noon on Saturday.

*St. Vincent:* General Post Office, Kingstown. Open 8.30 a.m. to 3 p.m. Monday to Friday, 8.30 to 11 a.m. Saturday.

*Grenada:* General Post Office, Carenage, St. George's. Open 8 a.m. to 4 p.m. Monday to Friday.

*Trinidad:* Main Post Office, Wrightson Road, Port-of-Spain. Open 8 a.m. to 4.30 p.m. Monday to Friday, 8 a.m. to noon on Saturday.

*Tobago:* Scarborough has a small post office; same hours as Trinidad.

If you don't know in advance where you'll be staying, you can have mail sent to the Postmaster-General, General Delivery, at the central post office of the island in question. But you should first inform the post office, which will then keep your mail.

**Stamps** are sold in post offices and hotels, sometimes at small shops, drugstores and mini-marts. Prices vary, but postage is very reasonable compared with rates elsewhere.

**Telephone**

*Barbados:* Telephone service is generally efficient on Barbados. International calls can be dialled direct from most phones, or you can get a connection from your hotel room through the hotel operator, or by dialling 118 to contact the local overseas operator. There are sufficient call-boxes (small, plastic egg-shaped booths) in Bridgetown, at the airport and in some other towns. Public phones operate like those in the U.K., and dialling instructions are given in English.

*Trinidad and Tobago:* Avoid making international calls when possible. You may wait two hours or more for a connection even to a neighbouring island. It's easier to send a telex (better hotels have a telex system). There are a few public telephones. If you find one, insert a coin, wait for the tone and dial.

*St. Lucia, St. Vincent, Grenada:* St. Lucia has direct international dialling. Elsewhere phone service is usually fairly efficient when conducted from a hotel room through the operator. But, as in Trinidad, you may have to wait for overseas calls. There aren't many public telephones, and they're often out of order.

**Telegrams, telex.** Most hotels will send telegrams, some have their own telexes. Night letter rates are usually cheaper. Main telex/telegram offices:

*Barbados:* Cable and Wireless. Lower Broad Street, Bridgetown, tel. 429-4852. Open Monday to Friday 7 a.m. to 7 p.m., Saturday 7 a.m. to 1 p.m. Another office in Wildey, St. Michael, is open 24 hours.

*St. Lucia:* Cable and Wireless, Bridge Street, Castries, tel. 23301. Open 7 a.m. to 8 p.m. Monday to Saturday, 8 to 10 a.m. on Sunday; closed on holidays.

*St. Vincent:* Cable and Wireless, Halifax Street, Kingstown, tel. 71901. Open 7 a.m. to 7 p.m. Monday to Saturday, 8 a.m to noon on Sunday and holidays.

*Grenada:* Cable and Wireless, Mercury House, Carenage, tel. 2201. Open 7 a.m. to 7 p.m. Monday to Saturday, 4 to 6 p.m. on Sunday and holidays.

*Trinidad:* Textel, 1 Edward Street, Port-of-Spain, tel. 62-54431. Open 24 hours a day for international telex and telegraph services.

*Tobago:* Textel, Main Street, Scarborough. Open during office hours.

**COMPLAINTS.** If you feel you've been wronged, go first to the manager or owner of the establishment in question (restaurant, hotel, car hire agency, etc.). Your next resort is the local tourist board; for addresses, island by island, see Briefing section at the end of each chapter. Police usually deal with criminal offences, rather than complaints.

**C** On certain islands, there are hotel associations which sort out hotel/restaurant complaints:

Barbados Hotel Association, Bush Hill Garrison, Bridgetown, tel. 426–5041

Trinidad Hotel Association, Hilton Hotel, Port-of-Spain, tel. 62-43065

Grenada Hotel Association, P.O. Box 440, St. George's, tel. 4475

**CONVERTER CHARTS.** For fluid and distance measures, see p. 116. The islands are slowly changing over to the metric system.

**Temperature**

**Length**

**Weight**

**CRIME and THEFT.** As elsewhere, crime is on the rise in the Southern Caribbean. Take the usual precautions, and avoid bringing valuable jewellery to the islands. If you must, store it and other valuables (money, passport) in a hotel safe. Lock your room at all times, including the door that leads to the terrace. Do not leave valuables unattended on the beach.

The streets of the larger towns are best avoided at night, especially if you're alone or not accompanied by local people. Muggings and street theft, though infrequent, do occur. However romantic and tempting the beach may look after dark, single women and couples should not venture out alone on certain parts of these islands. Ask your hotel bartender, reception clerk or manager for advice before taking a late-night stroll.

**CUSTOMS and ENTRY FORMALITIES.** When you enter each island-nation, general duty-free rules apply. You may bring in about a quart or litre of wine or spirits, 200 cigarettes or 250 grammes of tobacco or up to 50 cigars, and any personal effects for immediate use as a tourist.

The following chart shows which duty-free items you may bring back home with you:

| Into: | Cigarettes | Cigars | Tobacco | Spirits | Wine |
|---|---|---|---|---|---|
| Australia | 200 | or 250 g. | or 250 g. | 1 l. | or 1 l. |
| Canada | 200 | and 50 | and 900 g. | 1.1 l. | or 1.1 l. |
| N. Zealand | 200 | or 50 | or ½ lb. | 1 qt. | and 1 qt. |
| S. Africa | 400 | and 50 | and 250 g. | 1 l. | and 1 l. |
| U.K.* | 200 | or 50 | or 250 g. | 1 l. | and 2 l. |
| U.S.A. | 200 | and 100 | and ** | 1 l. | or 1 l. |

\* For items purchased in a duty-free shop.
\*\* No restriction for personal use only.

Certain islands (Barbados, St. Lucia, St. Vincent, Grenada) do not require passports for citizens of the U.S., U.K. or Canada, though you must present a valid proof of citizenship (birth certificate, voter's registration card, etc.) But a passport is always the best identification, and is required on Trinidad-Tobago. Citizens of other countries must have passports, though the islands do not usually require visas (enquire at your tourist office or airline company). You must also present an on-going or return ticket upon arrival on each island.

Recently, health authorities on Barbados and Grenada have required a yellow fever vaccination certificate (or you can be vaccinated in the area) if you have travelled through an infected area. This vaccination is also officially recommended on Trinidad (a few cases were reported recently).

Customs and immigration officials always ask how long you plan to stay on the island you're entering. You are usually allowed a visit of to 6 months without a special visa. If you're travelling to Trinidad-Tobago, you must include both islands when you mention your length of stay. Be advised that changing a tourist visa in the Caribbean can be an administrative headache.

**D** **DRIVING\*.** Shipping your own car to the islands is probably not worth the trouble. On the major islands there's no problem about hiring a car. All of the islands except Trinidad-Tobago (where you need an International Driving Permit) require you to purchase a temporary visitor's driving permit.

**Driving conditions.** As in Great Britain, driving is on the left. Roads are almost uniformly difficult compared to the U.S., U.K. or Canada. They can be narrow and pot-holed, with drainage ditches on either side. Mountain roads are full of hairpin bends, so it's a good idea to blow your horn before the bend. Watch out for pedestrians and animals in the road. You may also come upon an occasional lorry (truck) taking up too much of the available road space. Drive with caution—even hired cars usually don't have seat belts.

**Road signs.** There are a few stop-lights on the larger islands. Some international pictograph signs indicate stop, yield right-of-way, do not enter, etc., but these are not numerous. Nor are road signs (except on Barbados, where towns are relatively well-marked). To find your way when driving, navigate with the best road maps you can buy. You might see a few signs in kilometres—this chart will help you make the conversion:

| km | 0 | 1 | 2 | 3 | 4 | 5 | 6 | 8 | 10 | 12 | 14 | 16 |
|----|---|---|---|---|---|---|---|---|----|----|----|----|
| miles | 0 | ½ | 1 | 1½ | 2 | | 3 | 4 | 5 | 6 | 7 | 8 | 9 |

**Fuel.** Prices vary a lot, and as elsewhere, are rapidly increasing. But on Trinidad-Tobago, petrol (gasoline) will probably remain a bargain for awhile, since Trinidad is a petroleum-producing country. Petrol is sometimes sold by the litre. Here are the various fluid-measure equivalents:

| imp. gals. | 0 | 5 | 10 |
|------------|---|---|----|
| litres | 0 | 5 | 10 | 20 | 30 | 40 | 50 |
| U.S. gals. | 0 | 5 | 10 |

**Parking regulations.** Parking is allowed wherever there is space, except when specifically prohibited. Port-of-Spain (Trinidad) has a few car parks, but in most Caribbean towns you just have to look for space. There are no parking meters. The police may ask you to move your car, but at present there are no heavy fines for parking in the wrong place.

**Speed limits.** These are sometimes marked. On a few wide Trinidadian roads, the maximum is 50 m.p.h. But you'll find that you cannot safely go much faster than 30 m.p.h. on most roads, and that town traffic generally moves along at about 15–20 m.p.h. Note that speed limits, when posted, are strictly enforced on Barbados.

**Breakdowns.** Should misfortune occur, you'll usually have to rely on local people or the police for help. If you're hiring a car, the company is responsible for any problems you may have. The Trinidad Automobile Association has a few teams of cruising mechanics who normally help anybody in trouble on the road, whether a member of the association or not.

**EMBASSIES, CONSULATES, HIGH COMMISSIONS.** There are very few consular services on the islands. The largest offices are maintained on Barbados and Trinidad. Most countries are represented by honorary consuls (private citizens who will try to give assistance).

**Barbados.** Hours are roughly 8 a.m. to 4 or 5 p.m. Monday to Friday, with variations. If you are on an island without consular representation, you can ring Barbados if your country is represented here:

U.S.A.: United States Embassy, Canadian Imperial Bank of Commerce Building, Broad Street, Bridgetown, tel. 63574 (mornings only)

U.K.: British High Commission, Barclays Bank Building, Roebuck Street, Bridgetown, tel. 63525

Canada: Canadian High Commission, CDC Building, Culloden Road, St. Michael, tel. 93550

**Trinidad.** Opening hours are approximately 8 a.m. to 4.30 p.m. Monday to Friday. Some consulates close for a lunch break.

U.S.A.: United States Embassy, 15 Queen's Park West, Port-of-Spain, tel. 62-26371/26376

U.K.: British High Commission, 90 Independence Square, Port-of-Spain, tel. 62-52861

Canada: Canadian High Commission, 72 South Quay, Port-of-Spain, tel. 62-37254/34787

**St. Vincent** has little in the way of consulates. The Deputy British High Commissioner can be reached in Kingstown, tel. 71701.

**G**   **GUIDES.** There are very few private tour guides, though small group tours can easily be arranged through agencies and hotels. Taxi drivers can be reliable guides. To find a good one, ask the tourist board or your hotel reception clerk.

**H**   **HAIRDRESSERS and BARBERS\*.** Most hairdressing establishments cater to both men and women. They can be found in the better hotels and on the main shopping streets of large towns. Prices vary, and will be higher, for example, in an exclusive Barbados hotel than in a small shop on St. Lucia.

**HEALTH PRECAUTIONS.** A sun tan can make you look wonderful, but a bad burn could ruin your holiday and your skin... permanently. So take it easy at first, especially if you have fair skin. Use sun-screen creams and wear a hat. Start with a few minutes' exposure the first day, increasing gradually. The sun's burning rays are at their most powerful from 11.30 a.m. to 2.30 p.m.

After a very hot day, a long night of air-conditioning could give you a chill or cold. If you need air-conditioning, put it on the "low" setting and keep out of the draft.

Food presents no special problems, though you might avoid street-stand snacks if you have a delicate stomach. Try not to mix sun, pills and alcohol. When packing for your trip, don't forget an adequate supply of your favourite medications, including aspirin, an analgesic and something to soothe the stomach and combat diarrhoea. In any event, local drugstores sell aspirin and home remedies (some reminiscent of the old patent-medicine days).

**Insects.** Mosquitoes, gnats and sand flies are a prevalent nuisance, though not dangerous. Skin creams which repel insects are available at local pharmacies. You can burn mosquito coils in your hotel room if mosquitoes are a problem. If you request it, the maid will spray your room.

**Manchineel tree.** This tree, with its attractive, but highly poisonous green fruit, is found all over the islands, especially near beaches. Even the bark and leaves are extremely toxic. Do not stand under the tree or touch the apple, which is poisonous. Most manchineel trees are clearly labelled or painted with a red ring.

**Schistosomiasis parasite.** Also called bilharzia, this parasite causes a highly dangerous illness that is crippling or deadly. The parasite is car-

**118**

ried by snails that inhabit fresh-water ponds on some of the islands. Always ask your guide or a local resident if ponds or streams are safe before bathing or wading. After exposure to the parasite, it may take several weeks for symptoms to develop. If you have flu with chest pains after visiting the islands, be sure to tell your doctor where you have been.

**Urchins and coral.** When in the water, take care to avoid the prickly black sea-urchin. If you accidentally step on one, the best cure is to apply lime or lemon juice immediately. This helps to calcify the spines, which then work their way harmlessly out of the skin. Razor-sharp coral can pierce your skin in an instant, so wear tennis shoes or flippers when snorkelling. Treat coral cuts as you would any wound, with antiseptic, plus the healing power of fresh sea air.

**Snakes.** The deadly *fer-de-lance* has been seen in the interior of the volcanic islands, but is hardly ever encountered by tourists.

**Sharks.** These do roam the Caribbean and Atlantic, but you probably won't see any. Avoid swimming at night, and don't wear shiny objects underwater.

**HITCH-HIKING.** Some people hitch-hike, and there is no law against it. But it's not recommended. Obviously, if you have a car and meet somebody at the beach who needs a lift, you should use your discretion.

**HOTELS and ACCOMMODATION**★. Every sort of accommodation is available on the major islands, from the comfort of expensive luxury hotels to small, self-catering studio flats. Tourist boards and travel agents can furnish official lists.

Remember that high season rates (roughly December 15 to April 15) are considerably higher than prices from April to December. Reserve in advance, especially during high season. Tourist boards usually have a complete set of photo-brochures of the major hotels, plus lists of self-catering accommodation (not always that much of a saving, or very practical).

The various plans offered are:

EP: European Plan (room only)
CP: Continental Plan (room and breakfast)
AP: American Plan (room and three meals)
MAP: Modified American Plan (room, breakfast plus one other meal)

**H** Some hotels allow only AP or MAP systems during high season. MAP is quite popular, since it saves money and is practical, unless you're set on trying a lot of restaurants.

In some hotels, package-tour deals offer lower rates for the same quality. Guest-houses are usually very reasonable, though there are fewer amenities. There are flats and small houses to let in all price ranges, and some of them are moderately priced. All accommodation except for the most luxurious is somewhat less expensive on St. Lucia, St. Vincent and Grenada than the other islands.

On all islands, taxes are charged in hotels and guest-houses, and there is usually a service charge as well. Barbados (currently the most expensive) adds on taxes of 8%, plus 10% service.

Youth hostels and the YMCA or YWCA exist only on Trinidad and Barbados. These may be found in the phone book, or by writing to the tourist office.

Some addresses:

YMCA: Pinfold Street, Bridgetown, Barbados, tel. 63910
YWCA: Bradfield Country Road, St. Michael, Barbados, tel. 64953
Youth hostel: Worthing, Christ Church, Barbados, tel. 87477

**I** **INTER-ISLAND TRAVEL\*.** You can, of course, travel between the islands by hired yacht, complete with staff, food, champagne, etc. Many hire companies have branch offices in the U.S. You can also hire a speedboat with driver. Tour operators offer one- or two-day excursions using the local airlines. But if you'd like to get around by yourself:

**From Trinidad to Tobago:** Daily flights link Trinidad and Tobago (see Briefing p. 81). There is also an inexpensive night ferry, but the trip takes 6 hours and is not recommended for comfort.

**From St. Vincent to the Grenadines:** Mustique, Canouan, and Union Island have airstrips for small planes. Enquire at Arnos Vale Airport (St. Vincent) for scheduled, unscheduled and charter flights. A daily shuttle schooner for tourists leaves Kingstown for Bequia in the afternoon, returning the next morning. This service is inexpensive and reliable. Ferries are also available to the other major Grenadine islands, though not on a daily basis. The adventurous can also travel through the Grenadines by mail boat. The boat leaves twice a week from Kingstown in the morning, stopping several times in the Grenadines and arriving at Grenada in the evening.

**From Grenada to Carriacou and Petit Martinique:** Daily 10-minute flights link Grenada and Carriacou. Trading schooners sail regularly from St. George's Harbour (Grenada) to Carriacou; from there you can sail on to Petit Martinique (just 3 miles to the north-east).

**LANGUAGE.** The official language on all the islands covered in this book is English, spoken in a variety of accents. If you don't understand what's being said just ask. The person you're talking to will repeat more clearly. On St. Lucia (and to some extent on St. Vincent) the people speak a lilting French patois among themselves.

**LAUNDRY and DRY-CLEANING.** Hotels can take care of laundry efficiently. One-day service is always possible, but costs more. There are no launderettes except on Barbados, though some towns have quick-service laundry and dry-cleaning establishments (not necessarily cheaper than the hotels). Prices vary according to where you are—they are usually higher on Barbados, lower on Tobago, Grenada, St. Vincent and St. Lucia.

**LOST PROPERTY.** For lost property, ask at the hotel or establishment where you misplaced the item. If you've left something on a bus, check with the local transport board. As a last resort, you could try the police station.

**MAPS.** Sometimes hotels furnish basic maps free, and tourist boards usually do so as well. The quality of maps varies according to the country. The St. Vincent tourist board charges a small fee for a top-notch survey map. The Trinidad-Tobago tourist boards also have very good maps. A general map of St. Lucia is available in bookstores, and the tourist board gives out a small map. On Barbados the tourist office map is rather sketchy, but an excellent survey map is available at a kiosk across from the BWIA office in Independence Square, Bridgetown.

**MEDICAL CARE.** (See also Briefing section under each island for emergencies, hospital.) The islands have adequate to good medical facilities and physicians especially on Barbados. Hotels or the tourist board can recommend a doctor or dentist. You can also look in the classified section of the phone book.

Chemists' (pharmacy) opening hours vary; some are open 7 days a week, though there is almost no 24-hour service. For pharmacies open in the evening, ask at your hotel desk or consult the local newspaper or phone book.

Here are a few pharmacies usually open after regular hours:

**Trinidad:** Alchemists' Drug Store, 57 Duke Street, Port-of-Spain, tel. 62-32718

**Tobago:** Dove Drugs, Burnett Street, Scarborough, tel. 639–2976

**St. Lucia:** Marshall's Pharmacy, Corner Brazil and Broglie Streets, Castries, tel. 22806

**Grenada:** Benoit's Pharmacy, Carenage, St. George's, tel. 3174

## MONEY MATTERS

**Currency.** Various currencies are in use on the islands. See the Briefing section at the end of each chapter.

**Banks and Currency Exchange.** The general rule is that banks are open from 8 a.m. to noon or 1 p.m. weekdays, later on Friday afternoons. Banks often shut for a half-day before major holidays. For specific hours, see island Briefings. Banks almost always have currency exchange windows.

The most acceptable form of payment is U.S. (or Canadian) dollars in traveller's cheques. You will usually need a passport or driver's licence for identification. Traveller's cheques are negotiable almost anywhere. Banks give the best rate of exchange, but in many cases you can get almost as good a rate at your hotel desk. Enquire as to how the rate compares with the bank's; hotels usually give an honest answer.

**Credit Cards and Traveller's Cheques.** Major credit cards are widely accepted throughout the islands by most hotels, better restaurants and shops, including duty-free shops at the airports (depending on the airport and type of purchase). Traveller's cheques are also accepted, preferably those in U.S. dollars.

**Prices.** As elsewhere, inflation is on the rise. However, prices are still reasonable compared with big cities in the U.S., Canada and Europe or European resort towns. In general Barbados and Trinidad tend to be more expensive than the other islands in the area.

There are some extraordinary bargains, such as petrol (gasoline) on Trinidad-Tobago. Beware of French wines, which can cost more than spirits and a lot more than local rum. Some locally made beers are also quite good and inexpensive.

Hotels and restaurants vary in price, but generally you'll find that for higher prices you do get better quality. Visiting the islands on package deals and especially during the low season (April 15–December 15) can mean considerable savings.

**PETS.** Few people bring pets on Caribbean holidays, due to strict government regulations. On Barbados, for example, visiting animals must undergo six months of isolation before being allowed into the country.

**PHOTOGRAPHY.** You can buy major brands of film, but it's best to bring your own, since supplies can be limited and prices are high. There are fast-development services on the larger islands, especially for black-and-white and transparencies. But in most cases, development is cheaper back home.

To ensure good colour transparencies in the blazing sunlight, you must use a skylight or similar filter. You'll probably get best seashore and outdoor results late in the afternoon.

People (especially children) are usually cooperative about having their pictures taken. But always ask first, and offer some small change if it seems this would be appreciated. Some people react in a hostile way if you try to photograph them. Islanders are proud, and you should respect their dignity.

Be sure to enquire whether security checks are made by X-ray, which can be harmful to undeveloped film.

**POLICE.** Each town, city and parish on the islands has a police station, and local people can always direct you to the nearest one. Police uniforms are "British-tropical", usually navy-blue trousers or shorts, grey shirts and white safari hats or helmets. The harbour police of Barbados dress in costumes right out of Gilbert and Sullivan. Once in a while you might spot a policeman directing traffic, but this is a rare sight on the islands. For police phone numbers, see various Briefing sections.

**R** **RADIO and TV.** Most radio programmes are in English. In addition to local offerings, programmes from Canada, the U.S. and BBC are broadcast on medium- or short-wave frequencies. A few French programmes from Martinique are transmitted to other islands.

Only Trinidad and Barbados have TV, consisting of a limited selection of programmes, mostly in black-and-white and mainly from the U.S.

Radio and TV stations are generally government-operated, and their shows feature local political chit-chat, some international news and music. Radios in hotel rooms pick up a few local stations with a limited selection of music. At present, there are few TV sets in hotel rooms.

**RELIGIOUS SERVICES.** Anglicans and Roman Catholics are in the majority on the islands. Methodist, Baptist and Seventh-Day Adventist churches, Hindu temples, synagogues and mosques point out the diversity of faiths in the Caribbean, especially on Trinidad and Barbados. For addresses and times of services, check with local newspapers, your hotel desk or the tourist office.

**T** **TAXIS\*.** As there are no meters, you should agree on a price with your driver before taking a taxi. In principle, taxi fares are set by the government of each island according to the mileage covered; in practice, you might hear some rather varied fares for the same distance on the same island. Before taking a taxi, ask at your hotel desk about the correct fare. You can also consult the tourist board office or the airport information officer before taking a taxi to a hotel.

Taxis are not always indicated as such, but you'll probably recognize drivers frequenting promising locations. On some islands, the word "taxi" is clearly marked on the windshield (windscreen). On Barbados, taxi licence plates have a small number 591 in addition to the regular number. On other islands, you will see "H" (for hire car) on the plate.

Drivers often double as guides. If you want to be sure of having a good one, reserve a day or so in advance through your hotel desk or the tourist office. You don't have to tip taxi drivers, though a 10% tip is always appreciated, especially if your driver has been giving you advice or acting as a guide.

The shared-taxi service that operates around Port-of-Spain on Trinidad and on Tobago proves a lot less expensive than a regular taxi. There are certain designated stops; be sure to signal the taxi when you **124** see it approaching.

**TIME DIFFERENCE.** The islands stay on Atlantic Standard Time all year. This is one hour ahead of Eastern Standard Time and four hours behind GMT. The U.S. east coast and the islands are on the same time when Daylight Savings Time is in effect.

| Winter time chart | | | | |
|---|---|---|---|---|
| Los Angeles | Chicago | New York | **Islands** | London |
| 8 a.m. | 10 a.m. | 11 a.m. | **noon** | 4 p.m. |

**TIPPING.** A 10% service charge is often included in hotel and restaurant bills. If not added to bills, tip waiter 10–15%. Taxi drivers also get 10–15%, bellboys and porters about U.S.$0.25 per bag.

**TOILETS.** There are very few public facilities on the islands. They're usually marked "public conveniences" with a silhouette or a sign indicating "men" or "women".
   Airports always have toilet facilities, but not all of them are inviting. The new Barbados airport has good lavatory facilities that are so far very clean.

**WATER.** Tap water in hotels, restaurants and flats is safe on all the islands. It tastes quite good, especially on Barbados. The islands sometimes have problems with plumbing (such as Tobago during heavy rains). Water in hotel rooms may be turned off. The hotel will give you safe drinking water if this happens. You can buy bottled mineral water, but it is rather expensive.

T

W

# Index

An asterisk (*) next to a page number indicates a map reference.

**Barbados**   9*, 17–30, 19*
  Andromeda Gardens   19*, 27
  Animal Flower Cave   19*, 28
  Ashford Bird Park   19*, 25–26
  Barbados Museum
    (Bridgetown)   19*, 23–24
  Bathsheba   19*, 26–27
  Bridgetown   9*, 19*, 20–24
  Chalky Mount   19*, 27
  Cherry Tree Hill   19*, 28
  Codrington College   19*, 25
  Crane Beach   19*, 24
  Farley Hill (plantation
    house)   19*, 28
  Gun Hill   27
  Harrison's Cave   28
  Holetown   19*, 27–28
  Markets and shopping   22,
    89–90
  Morgan Lewis Windmill   19*,
    29
  Nicholas Abbey (plantation
    house)   19*, 29
  North Point   19*, 28
  Paradise Beach   19*, 27
  Payne's Bay   19*, 27
  Potteries, The   27
  Practical information   30
  St. Ann's Fort   24
  St. John's Church   19*, 26
  Sam Lord's Castle   19*, 24–25
  Sandy Lane Bay   19*, 27
  Six Men's Bay   19*, 28
  Speightstown   19*, 28
  Villa Nova (plantation house)
    19*, 25
  Welchman Hall Gully   19*, 28

Bequia   9*, 41*, 49–50
Boating   85–86

Calypso music   94
Canouan   41*, 50
Carnival   92–93, 96–97
Carriacou   9*, 53*, 58, 61

Drinks   105

Fishing   85
Food   98–105

Golf   77, 86
**Grenada**   9*, 52–58, 53*, 60
  Botanical Gardens and Zoo
    (St. Georges's)   54–55
    Concorde Falls   58
  Dougaldston Estate   53*, 57
  Gouyave (Charlotte Town)
    53*, 57
  Grand Anse Beach   53*, 56
  Grand Etang (volcano)   53*,
    58
  Grenville   53*, 58
  Lance aux Epines   53*, 56
  Levera Bay   53*, 58
  Markets and shopping   55–56,
    90
  Morne du Sauteurs   54, 57–58
  Point Jeudy   53*, 56
  Point Saline   53*, 56
  Practical information   60
  Prickly Point   53*, 56
  Royal Drive   50

St. George's   9*, 53*, 54–56
Sauteurs   53*, 57
Westerhall Point   53*, 56
Woburn   56
**Grenadines**
Grenada's ~   53*, 58, 60, 121
St. Vincent's ~   9*, 41*
   49–51, 121

Horse riding   86–87

Mustique (island)   9*, 41*, 50

Nightlife   97–98

Palm Island   41*, 50
Petit Martinique (island)   53*,
   61
Petit St. Vincent (island)   41*, 50
Petroglyphs   46
Prices   108

Restaurants, see Food

**St. Lucia**   9*, 31–40, 33*
Anse la Raye   33*, 36
Anse Cochon   33*, 36
Canaries   33*, 36
Cap Estate   33*, 35
Castries   9*, 33*, 33–35
Choc Beach   33*, 35
Choiseul   33*, 38–39
Cul de Sac   33*, 35–36
Dennery   33*, 39
Fort Charlotte   33*, 34–35
Gros Islet   33*, 35
Laborie   33*, 38–39
Marigot Bay   33*, 36
Markets and shopping   33, 90
Micoud   33*, 39

Morne Fortuné   33*, 34–35
Moule à Chique   39
Pigeon Island   33*, 35
Pitons (volcanos)   33*, 35, 36
Practical information   40
Soufrière (town)   33*, 36
Soufrière (volcano)   35, 38
Sulphur Springs   33*, 36–37
Vieux Fort   33*, 39
Vigie Beach   33*, 35
**St. Vincent**   9*, 41*, 41–49, 51
Barrouallié   41*, 46
Belvedere Point   47
Botanic Gardens
   (Kingstown)   44
Fort Charlotte   41*, 44
Kingstown   9*, 41*, 43–44
Layou Bay   41*, 46
Markets and shopping   43, 90
Mesopotamia/Marriaqua
   Valley   41*, 47
Pleasant, Mount   46
Practical information   51
Questelles   44
Richmond Beach   41*, 46
Soufrière (volcano)   41*,
   48–49
Young Island   41*, 46
Shopping   88–92
Sports   82–87
Steelband music   94
Swimming   83–84

Tennis   86
**Tobago**   9*, 61, 74*, 74–81
Arnos Vale Hotel   78
Buccoo Reef   77
Castara Bay   74*, 78
Charlotteville   74*, 78
Englishman's Bay   74*, 78
Fort William   77
Grafton Estate   78

Great Courland Bay
  Monument   *78*
Little Tobago   *74\*, 80*
Man O'War Bay   *74\*, 78*
Mount Irvine Bay Hotel   *77*
Parlatuvier   *74\*, 78*
Pigeon Peak   *74\*, 78*
Pigeon Point   *74\*, 76–77*
Plymouth   *74\*, 77*
Practical information   *81*
Scarborough   *9\*, 74\*, 75–76*
Shopping   *91–92*
Speyside   *74\*, 80*
Tobago Forest Reserve   *74\*,
  78*
Tobago Cays   *41\*, 50*
**Trinidad**   *9\*, 61, 62–73, 63\*, 81*
  Aripo Caves   *63\*, 72*
  Asa Wright Nature Centre
    *63\*, 71*
  Blue Basin   *63\*, 69–70*
  Botanic Gardens (Port-of-
    Spain)   *68–69*

Caroni Bird Sanctuary   *63\*,
  69*
Chaguanas   *63\*, 71*
Cocos Bay   *63\*, 73*
Fort George   *63\*, 69*
Maracas Beach   *63\*, 71*
Markets and shopping   *67, 71,
  91–92*
Mayaro Bay   *63\*, 73*
National Museum and Art
  Gallery (Port-of-Spain)
  *66\*, 67*
Pitch Lake   *63\*, 72–73*
Port-of-Spain   *9\*, 63\*, 64–69,
  66\**
Practical information   *81*
Queen's Park Savannah (Port-
  of-Spain)   *66\*, 67–69*
Sangre   *63\*, 73*
Skyline Drive   *63\*, 71*
Valencia   *63\*, 73*

Union (island)   *41\*, 50*